the
mountain
knows
the
mountain

the mountain knows the mountain

a fire watch diary

philip connors

SPECIAL GUEST APPEARANCES BY
mónica ortiz uribe AND
bobby byrd

HIGH ROAD BOOKS
albuquerque

© 2025 by Philip Connors
Afterword © 2024 by the Estate of Bobby Byrd
All rights reserved. Published 2025
Printed in the United States of America

ISBN 978-0-8263-6834-8 (cloth)
ISBN 97-8-08263-6835-5 (electronic)

Library of Congress Control Number: 2025932271

Founded in 1889, the University of New Mexico sits on the traditional
homelands of the Pueblo of Sandia. The original peoples of New
Mexico—Pueblo, Navajo, and Apache—since time immemorial have
deep connections to the land and have made significant contributions
to the broader community statewide. We honor the land itself and those
who remain stewards of this land throughout the generations and also
acknowledge our committed relationship to Indigenous peoples. We
gratefully recognize our history.

Cover illustration by Isaac Morris
Designed by Isaac Morris
Composed in Cormorant Garamond
No artificial intelligence was used in the creation of this book.

For Nina,
who lit a match in the dark,

and Lee,
who fed the flame

All true paths lead through mountains.
—GARY SNYDER

The notebook is the perfect literary form for an eternal student, someone who has no subject or, rather, whose subject is "everything."
—SUSAN SONTAG

Contents

a few words by way of a preface   XI

APRIL   1

MAY   27

JUNE   47

JULY   77

AUGUST   113

AFTERWORD
a visit to the mountain, one year later   139
    Bobby Byrd

POSTSCRIPT
the last letter   159

acknowledgments   175
selected sources   177
contributors   179
permissions   181

a few words by way of a preface

Beginning in the summer of 2002, I worked each year for several months on a mountain in New Mexico. There I recorded weather and kept watch for wildfires as an employee of the United States Forest Service. Just prior to what would have been my fifteenth consecutive year as a lookout, I underwent two surgeries, one on each hip. Afterward I felt and moved like a broken marionette. I feared my lookout days were done. I sensed my identity threaten to disintegrate. And of course I dreamed from a distance of the mountain.

A year passed. My health slowly improved; the mountain beckoned once more. Having missed an entire fire season there, I felt eager to reacquaint myself with the moods and mysteries of the place. I bought a notebook whose pages were meant to accrue observations of weather and creatures and to record the twists and turns of my mind under conditions of solitude. In certain years I had been quite thorough about this, in others less so, but always I had scribbled. As the notebooks filled across a decade and more, I sometimes wondered whether I could find new insights about the experience.

I knew, as I prepared for my return, that the rhythms of the mountain had carried on quite indifferently to my absence, though they had been a continuing presence in my memory. In tribute to the solace they had given me during my convalescence, I resolved to find fresh language for old rituals. Perhaps the way to say more was to find new ways to say less.

The results, if squinted at from a distance, bear some resemblance to a form practiced by Japanese haiku poets of the seventeenth, eighteenth, and nineteenth centuries: the *haibun*, a blend of poetry and prose. Haibun often took the form of a diary in which poems acted as a subtle expansion of, or counterpoint to, passages of prose that were themselves poetic. Kobayashi Issa's *The Spring of My Life* represents one notable example, but the most beloved of all haibun remains Matsuo Bashō's *Narrow Road to the Interior*, alternately translated as *Narrow Road to the Far North*, based on a journey he made from Edo (now Tokyo) through the northern provinces of Honshu in 1689.

My own effort, it should be admitted, represents an accidental foray in the form. Unlike the classics of haibun, my notebook does not detail a long journey or an encounter with a new place. Instead it marks a return to the familiar. I didn't set out to create a specific effect or follow a particular template. I merely strove to represent what I saw and felt over the course of five months of mountain sitting. During those months I discovered a poetic impulse for the first time in my life, and though fearful I did not possess the artistry to honor it, I tried anyway. Sometimes that's all we can do. Try. And be true to the music in our minds when experience elicits the urge to sing.

I should say that, despite all the talk of haiku and haibun, no specialized knowledge is required to appreciate this chronicle. All that's needed is a mind as attuned to nonhuman beauty as

a few words by way of a preface

mine was when I put foot in front of foot on my way up the mountain, notebook stuffed in my pack. I should also say that I am not, repeat not, a government spokesperson, despite having long been a government employee. These are my own private thoughts and observations, for whatever they are worth. They already have the slight flavor of a relic from a bygone era; with the Forest Service and the rest of the federal civil service under assault as this book goes to press, the work described here is likely soon to be relegated to the dustbin of history.

I will keep writing about the work until I'm dragged off my tower and ordered to leave, and I'll probably publish some of what I write, despite a New York editor once scolding me that I had written my lookout book and was only entitled to one. The presumptuousness of his view offended the sanctity of my creative life and made me resolve to write not just one or two such books, but four or five: books that examine the work and the place I do it through the lens of celebration, lamentation, poeticization, novelization . . . To me this feels utterly natural because the mountain keeps changing, the land keeps evolving, and the deep map of place that is my writerly project can always stand an update.

During the seasons that inspired my haibun notebook— spring and summer 2017—the mountain became a presence in the life of my spouse, Mónica. One year later it entered into the life of my friend Bobby. I am happy to include their voices and views of the mountain alongside mine. Every mountain deserves more than one praise song. Herein you will find three.

april

The mountain has been here for thirty-four million years, give or take. It emerged from within a great volcanic caldera, and the welded tuff that is its rock can only be moved with dynamite, as the builders of the old outhouse attest. This gives the place a flavor of eternity. My absence from it for the past twenty months amounts to something less than a blink in time; the season ahead will be but another half blink. Within that half blink, I resolve to absorb the mountain's energies to the utmost. I am blessed to be here, and I wish to honor all it gives of life and light.

> craving solitude
> life with my head in the clouds
> voila   fire lookout

I arrived this afternoon with cold, wet feet after a snowy trudge up the north slope—so cold I didn't pause to admire the view. Rounding the cabin, intent on getting inside and starting a fire, I noticed my favorite tree partially in ruin. It had split in half vertically along the length of its trunk. One half of it still stood, rooted in the rock of the mountain; the other half lay on the ground, broken limbs scattered about, needles still green. It had always been a double-trunk tree, a white pine forty feet tall with two sturdy boles forking about ten feet above the roots. A heavy snowfall over the winter made the split between the forks complete. Along the fracture, amid the heartwood, I found evidence of pack rat habitation: feces and a nest. There must have been a crevice where the parallel boles diverged, and the pack rats made use of it, weakening the tree in the process.

There are other trees I love and often visit in various places on the flanks of the peak—bigger ones, older ones, mainly Douglas firs—but the snow-damaged pine stood fifty feet south of the tower, making it the tree I've looked at more than any other in my life. I often stared up at its crown from my hammock. Still can, in fact, since the nail on which I hang one end of the hammock remains sunk in the portion of the tree that's still upright. It occurs to me that maybe I'm a little like the tree: neither of us quite what we used to be, but still hanging on despite our wounds.

It was a proud tree, or so it always seemed to me, dense with needles, a favorite of the squirrels and the Clark's nutcrackers for its enormous seed cones. Can the standing half survive in the long run? Perhaps. But eventually rot will set in and spread through the exposed heartwood, and one day the standing half will fall, joining its twin on the ground . . . Such are the fateful conjectures and minor sorrows that occupy my first night here, a night I had imagined containing only joy at my reunion with the mountain.

april

how peculiar
mourning a dismembered tree
like a lost brother

Another twenty-first-century springtime spent in nineteenth-century fashion: a romantic in search of the sublime. Given the drift of the culture, might I be forgiven an attraction to the archaic?

Really, though, why continue in this line of work, forestry technician/lookout, pay grade GS–04, temporary seasonal? My bank balance after a year of infirmity and another winter unemployed is $496.72. Why not move on and improve my prospects—a year-round job, a living wage, a pension to retire on—after a decade and a half of watching for fire in what's left of the New Mexico wilderness?

I could give many answers. My love of the landscape. My delight in its creaturely life. My pursuit of beauty and happiness, nowhere more fruitful than here. My need for a space in which to think and write untethered to the hive mind. My aversion to spending more minutes in an office than days on the payroll in any given year, for any employer at all.

Or maybe I should cop to simple vanity, aware there's a certain cachet to saying, "I live on a mountain."

In a more tactile way, the reasons are these: I wish to touch the source of the water I drink. I prefer to feel intimate with the energy that warms me. Nostalgia, one might charge. To which I can only reply: spot on, dude! I had the luck to grow up drinking sweet well water—vestigial glaciers—untainted by the taste of chlorine, and my family heated our farmhouse with wood in the Minnesota winters. Reenacting versions of these experiences is conducive, as is so much else here, to calming the mind and discerning the real. Part of what's alienating about life in the lurid concrete valleys—beyond the aggressive ugliness of our built environments, which too often provoke aggression and ugliness in me—is the severed link between our well-being and what sustains it. Down there, water flows out of a tap, heat from an HVAC system, a sense of social worth through a screen. Colossal achievements, no doubt, but will the infrastructure that sustains them endure, and not in the end prove ruinous for life on Earth? I wouldn't bet a nickel on it. The dwindling aquifer, the fracked petroleum that feeds the power plant that feeds the server farm that keeps the screens humming: these stay out of mind by being kept out of sight. Things we cannot see or touch we find hard to credit, and when we're estranged from the sources of our comfort, we tend to turn profligate. Here I listen to rain trickle through the gutters into the cistern, a weapon of war repurposed—

> buried on its side
> guided-missile container
> finally aimed right

—and I honor the tree whose limbs, dismembered by my own effort, feed my wood stove on frigid nights. Little things, maybe,

april

but not nothing. Transcending elemental limits has been the goal of profiteers for centuries, and the fruits of their efforts have made for a comfortable run for some of us. But any culture not sociopathic at its core tends to make a sacrament of life-sustaining consumption. Ours has made of it a thoughtless sacrilege. A few of us ought to live simply in contact with the vanishing things, an act of atonement and solidarity. Best we be the sort of person who secretly wishes to vanish too, or maybe just the sort of person who knows what Gary Snyder meant when he spoke of "how walking the landscape can become both ritual and meditation." Walking here is my ritual, my meditation, my atonement, my act of solidarity with my fellow creatures. It is my sacrament and my spiritual practice.

As for my work with words, I recall a line from Mary Oliver: "If I have any lasting worth, it will be because I have tried to make people remember what the Earth is meant to look like." So few places resemble how they were meant to look, fewer all the time. This place, the Gila Wilderness, is one of the best we've got left. What luck to live here for another season of fire.

> Returning to a high place,
> a trespasser on a wild space
> where ego melts in the sun
> & the bears turn and run
> as soon as they smell me:
> the proverbial bat in the belfry.

the mountain knows the mountain

I am reminded that about two weeks are required for the discomfort of solitude to fade after a winter amid the social scene. Even after all these years, I'm surprised by how foul I feel to be so suddenly alone. Maybe I've felt foul for months and am only now noticing, since feeling foul is ops normal in my winter home of El Paso, where the people are lovely, but border-surveilling helicopters menace the sky, police and ambulance sirens wail day and night, and the oil refinery fogs the air with pollution.

> unfit for cities
> allergic to life indoors
> a bear in a zoo

Or it could be the case that I've got a banal and predictable case of the ol' SAD—seasonal affective disorder—which will pass as the season turns. All I know is that writing a few words in this notebook feels like a chore, performed as much from habit and obligation as from inspiration. I want nothing more than to sleep the days away. I am strangely sluggish, as if I've spent the winter filling my pockets with rocks. I stare at repairs to the tower calling out for attention and think: not today. Maybe tomorrow. More likely next month, next year . . . I consider my manuscripts and preemptively judge them a squandering of time and a certain failure, mere egotism. I eat to console myself, eat some more. I walk the trails around the peak and find them littered with logs, overgrown with thorny locust, a pain (literally) to pass through. It's too cold to inhabit the tower comfortably, twenty-nine degrees at nine in the morning, wind gusts to twenty-five miles an hour and promise of higher as the day goes on.

the mountain knows the mountain

> dust devils dancing
> far off on the desert floor
> mistresses of wind

But hold on, cowboy. Why begin this notebook with a focus on the negative? Complaining about anything here is a squandering of time when my time is my own to do with as I please, as long as I look out the window every fifteen minutes. I am the luckiest white boy I know. I have the good fortune to live on a mountain with a view of two countries, four states (Texas, New Mexico, Arizona, Chihuahua), and two dozen distant ranges. I have two thousand gallons of rainwater at my disposal and an endlessly renewable supply of firewood at hand. The pantry is stocked from years past, food for a month, enough to last until the pack mules arrive with this year's groceries. I have coffee, my daily drug of choice, and a supply of propane to run the fridge and stove. Most importantly, I have the best seasonal job on the planet. My mind may wander wherever it likes. The weather will turn agreeable before long. The mountain will begin to share its splendors. The creatures will arrive in abundance: more birds, more mammals, more reptiles, more insects all the time. The tower will become my daylong residence; that astonishing expanse of mountains and desert out the windows will become a theater for my imagination, a playground for my optic nerves. I will, with some hesitation and more than a little difficulty, move through the process of opening my senses to the glories and sorrows of the landscape. I will stand agog before its dramas of weather

april

and wildfire. I will succumb to its seductions, surrender to its majesty and immensity. I will oscillate, for a little while, on the same wavelength as the Earth.

> another morning
> to & from the old outhouse
> the trail i know best

I have my chosen saplings I nurse with gray water. Dishwater, laundry water, mop water: all get parceled out among a few of my favorites, three Douglas firs, two ponderosas, and a limber pine. The one I've nursed the longest is now fifteen feet tall, and each appears healthy despite my going AWOL on them for a summer. Some future tree-ring scientist will be puzzled to discover healthy growth rings even in the drought years.

Trail work: a remedy for psychic malaise, the simple back and forth of a handsaw through wood. I've cleared fifteen trees along the last mile of trail to the lookout and dropped one precarious leaner. A couple of hours of work each evening and I am bequeathed a glow of accomplishment, a sense of satisfaction. What else can a person do, aside from clearing a path in the woods, that is useful to both humans and bears?

the mountain knows the mountain

> every two weeks
> money in my bank account
> nowhere to spend it

While digging a trail through the snow and ice for the mule packers to bring my supplies up the last bit of the north slope, I found a few strands of horse hair from last year's pack-out trip. They're just what I need to repair the crosshairs on the Osborne Fire Finder. Traditionally the crosshairs were fashioned using strands from a horse's tail. Some of my fellow lookouts still swear by them: the dark, well-defined lines, their crisp intersection. Here they shall remain in use, thanks to my serendipitous discovery in the snow.

    Also:

> found the tin bathtub
> halfway down the mountainside
> as if it had plans

Why in springtime does the river run blue with snowmelt, so much bluer than with summer rain? I suspect it has to do with

april

time. A snowflake spends more time dancing through sky than a raindrop does, and therefore gathers more sky into itself on its wayward journey to Earth.

> geeking out on clouds
> a sweet way to fill the hours
> bean soup on the stove

Hidden inside a makeshift cairn on the mountain for more than a decade now has been a small tin box with a note tucked inside. I discovered it one year by accident, a small totem of someone else's connection with this mountain. The note, written in green ink, resides inside a plastic bag with the word "Toto" written on it in black marker. The note reads as follows: "The ashes of our wonderful dog Toto are spread here. Toto loved to hike here. He loved snow." On the reverse side of the note is written: "We love you, Papa and Momma." Each year, when I return to the mountain, I make sure the tin box is still there, hidden amid the rocks. I open it and read the note, read as well the sticker on the rust-speckled bottom of the tin—

Animal Health Specialty
Services of Albuquerque
6901 Second NW
Albuquerque NM 87107

—and surmise, once more, that Toto's ashes were delivered to his caretakers in the plastic bag tucked inside the tin. I imagine the ceremony that accompanied their spread on the mountain, the memories recounted, Toto's final return to a place he loved. And I hope that someday someone will do for me what Papa and Momma did for their dog. Bring me here as powder in a box and set me free on the wind.

> ashes from the stove
> tossed over the mountain's edge
> trial run for mine

For a fire lookout, planning begins before the season does. This notebook ought to contain a long entry from March on preparation and logistics; buying and packing supplies is a prerequisite to joining the payroll. I am talking about not just groceries (though mostly that), but reading material and all the various gear needed for 150 days, give or take, on a mountain five miles from a road and forty more to the nearest store. All must be well packed in boxes for a journey on the backs of mules, nothing loose or rattley that will spook the animals. For ease in balancing the load, each box should have a twin in size and weight. I stand on a bathroom scale with each box, adding or subtracting things as necessary. This process never fails to remind me that over the winter my own weight stabilizes at around 175 pounds. After a few weeks on the mountain, hiking in the off hours each evening, I'll be closer to my fighting weight of 157.

I typically pack around 600 pounds of food, books, and supplies: two-way radios, batteries, binoculars, paint, tools, window cleaner, typewriter, et cetera. Added to this are eight bottles of propane to run the cookstove and refrigerator, and two coolers full of apples, potatoes, carrots, onions, and tortillas—all of it together a full load for six mules.

And here they came up the trail today, my firefighter colleagues Hondo and Güero, each of them horseback, each leading a pack string. Christmas in April! We unloaded the panniers from the mules' backs, stacked the boxes on the porch, and caught up on our respective winter doings while they ate burritos for lunch. Then they climbed back in the saddle and waved *adios*, the last of my colleagues I will see here until I'm packed out in five months.

Some of what was in those boxes I had forgotten, having closed them up a month or more ago. Ricola lozenges. A collection of Robinson Jeffers poems. A new sun-shower bladder. Weird to be so surprised by your own intentions, your own plans.

I had never created a master list of groceries needed for a season on the hill. That changed this year as I noted inventory while stowing my food in the pantry. The list that resulted:

6 lb. steel-cut oats	*25 lb. bag sugar (hummingbird*
2 lb. rolled oats	*food)*
10 lb. pancake mix	*5 jars mayonnaise*
6 qt. maple syrup	*3 jars mustard*
4 lb. brown sugar	*3 jars ketchup*
10 lb. all-purpose flour	*1 bottle grapeseed oil*

the mountain knows the mountain

1 bottle olive oil
1 bottle canola oil
1 bottle balsamic vinegar
baking powder
baking soda
vanilla extract
black pepper
salt
cumin seeds
red pepper flakes
onion powder
garlic powder
lemon pepper
cumin powder
turmeric
Italian seasoning
5 jars peanut butter
big jar honey
12 cans pasta sauce
6 jars pesto sauce
2 jars tomato pesto
6 jars sun-dried tomatoes
6 jars artichoke hearts
6 boxes rotini pasta
8 lb. spaghetti noodles
2 bags vermicelli noodles
10 small cans tomato sauce

6 small cans tomato paste
6 cans diced tomatoes
20 cans pickled jalapeños
16 cans Herdez salsa
6 cans chipotle sauce
3 bottles Cholula sauce
1 jar Better Than Bouillon
4 cans Spam (traditional at
lookouts)
6 cans chicken
10 cans tuna
8 lb. coffee
big bag powdered milk
can powdered goat milk
5 lb. pitted dates
2 lb. raisins
1 lb. currants
12 mixed-fruit cups (with cherries)
16 cans garbanzos
16 cans corn
12 cans pickled beets
12 cans green olives
6 cans carrots
6 cans refried beans
2 lb. walnuts
1 lb. pecans
1 lb. almonds

april

2 bags white rice
1 lb. quinoa
2 lb. red lentils
1 lb. green lentils
bag of split peas
2 jars diced garlic
2 boxes graham crackers
10 boxes mac & cheese (Annie's white cheddar)
10 cans diced green chiles
1 box organic corn flakes (for Mónica's visits)
4 jars Kalamata olives
5 jars green curry paste
10 cans coconut milk

curry bouillon cubes
bottle of rice vinegar
bottle of siracha
bottle of soy sauce
1 lb. dry hummus mix
2 lb. pinto beans
4 bags dried soup mix
2 lb. freeze-dried veggies
3 lb. veggie burger mix
green tea
mint tea
chamomile tea
honey
2 lb. dried blueberries

yellow-rumped warbler
ah to have a name so fine
yellow-rumped warbler

the mountain knows the mountain

Living in the middle of a two-hundred-square-mile burn scar, four years after the biggest fire ever to touch these mountains, means living amid the ruins of the forest I once knew. More dead trees stand than living ones, monuments to what was: a mixed-conifer forest of astonishing beauty on the high peaks. One by one the snags succumb. Every wind storm takes a few more. It is a cause for mourning and also a kind of privilege, even a responsibility, to live here among them. We are all, it would appear, destined to live amid the ruins of what we once knew and loved, especially if what we loved was an old-growth forest—our penance for being alive and sentient for this moment of climate chaos and systems collapse, and for being in our tiny way contributors to them. If I close my eyes and go back in time, I see it all again in my mind, a series of vivid scenes from a month-long inferno that reset life in these mountains forever after.

> jostled by beauty
> every which way i turn
> of course it would burn

> cataclysmic fire
> from cataclysmic lightning
> earth's oldest story

> charred snags etch the sky
> with delicate precision
> calligrapher's brush

the mountain knows the mountain

My obligation: bear witness as the wild world goes about its cycles of rejuvenation and renewal. Even out of disaster and destruction, life struggles for purchase, as the wolves of Chernobyl so vividly attest. Besides, someone should look with appreciation and pity upon a charismatic, fire-killed tree on the mountain's south slope. Someone ought to caress its bark and marvel at its spectral branches, twisted by wind for a century. Someone ought to note the presence of the dark-eyed junco hopping about the base of that snag, eating bugs of an early spring day. Someone should recognize that the gap under the bark where the cambium once pulsed with nutrients is now a hiding space for miller moths. By accident or fate, the someone in question turns out to be me. I am reminded of the eighth-century Chinese monk Han Shan, writing poems on Cold Mountain, and the dead tree of which he sang:

> People laugh at the gnarled remains,
> never thinking of the complex beauty of the grain within.
> Let the skin and flesh fall free . . .
> What's true, what's real, is there, inside.

dead snags all around
relics of the old forest
woodpecker condos

april

    fire-following moss
first spot of green in the char
    harbinger of life

    patient as beggars
gnarled & wizened as old saints
    the doug firs stand watch

Some days are so lovely—drinking coffee on the porch, making pancakes, scribbling in this notebook, reading a bit of a novel, cutting wood, watching mountains, clearing trail with an ax soaked in a bucket of water to make sure the bit doesn't slip off the handle, a trick I learned from a canny old Swede—that to make more of them than a list such as this would be to desecrate them. So let's leave it at that, say no more. Except:

    sixty-five steps up
afternoon of vigilance
    sixty-five steps down

Amid the din of the city in winter, when I remember the mountain, I think of it green from July rains, the meadow tinged with the deep blue of dayflowers. Or I recall those June days of a humming stillness, the only sound that of birdsong. My mind edits and rearranges the experience of living here to avoid recall of the first weeks, which represent a hazing ritual performed by the mountain on anyone bold enough to claim it as a home.

    Wind is the major trial, the droning flow of it, the remorseless battering of anything vertical: tree, tower, human. Blowing dust brings tears to the eyes. Blowing pollen from the junipers draws strings of mucus from the nose. Getting out of bed becomes an exercise of will. Overnight the temperature drops below freezing, some nights far below, into the teens. The mind becomes aware upon waking that building a fire in the wood stove is imperative, a chore to be performed in the absence of the heat the chore promises. Cold, stiff hands fumble for paper, kindling, a match. That moment—well after you've forgotten the warmth created by the cutting of firewood and just before the warmth created by the burning of it—is marked by a mild desperation: please, please let the first match catch . . .

      how to stay humble
      the mountain makes sure of it
        gusts to fifty-five

april

Reading old journals—to see how often I repeat myself, to confront past misperceptions and revise them, or just to laugh at my silly old self and all my pretensions—I find an entry from a decade ago that represents my attempt to explain, in thumbnail form, the history of fire in this place. I'm surprised to find it holds up okay, even though I couldn't see the scale of what was coming. I copy it here to feel the uncanny sensation of writing in my own voice even as the voice sounds strange, like an answering-machine message played back years later:

As a Forest Service lookout, I like to say that I am paid to watch trees. But I find myself increasingly intrigued by grass. From time immemorial, fire and grass worked in tandem here. Fires, some of them set by aboriginal people, moved through the grassy forest understory, only rarely torching in treetops. Fire kept the saplings in check, mostly sparing mature trees that were often centuries old. A slice from an ancient juniper trunk showcased at the Gila Cliff Dwellings National Monument shows in its tree-ring scars that fire burned around it, on average, every seven years going back centuries. Fire helped it thrive. Fire kept it healthy.

In 1826 one of the early Anglo arrivals in the region, James Ohio Pattie, claimed to have been "fatigued by the difficulty of getting through the high grass, which covered the heavily timbered bottom" of the Gila River canyon. The sheep and cattle that came afterward devoured that grass, trampled the stream banks, and disrupted the ancient fire regime. The streams saw beaver slaughtered for the whims of Eastern fashion. Beaver-dammed wetlands drained away, and with them went the previous abundance of water birds. On the overgrazed mesas, grass fires became less common; brush began to encroach on grasslands; piñon and juniper crept down the foothills. The Forest Service only exacerbated the trends with its arrival on the scene. Its goal became to put out every fire by ten o'clock the morning after the fire first appeared. That was the essence of the new forestry, the removal of a keystone ecological process. Fire suppression ensured that the conifers grew unchecked in the high elevations, crowding out the aspens, which love stand-re-placement fires. Brushy ladder fuels took hold in the forest understory, creating a flammable link to old-growth crowns. Over time, fires became harder to suppress, so the Forest Service responded with ever more military technology: tankers, chop-pers, bulldozers—a full-on, techno-industrial war on fire.

That began to change in the Gila National Forest in 1978. "Prescribed natural fires" became the preferred tool, started by lightning and allowed to burn within predetermined areas, mostly inside the wilderness, far from human settlements. The terminology later evolved into "wildland fire-use fires," then "wildland fire-use fires managed for resource benefit," because making its purpose obscure through the deployment of excessive verbiage is the US government way. But the basic principle held. Burn, baby, burn: that is now the mantra in the Gila, and for that reason among others—including its paucity of roads—this place is healthier than others like it in the West.

Does it resemble its optimum post-Pleistocene state? Not by any means. Still too many cows, too few fires. But much of what makes the Gila special remains unchanged over the centuries. Smoke overlaying the land and funneling into the canyons when the forest burns. The pulsing ebb and flood of an untamed river, trout in the deep pools of the headwaters.

april

A community of native flora still mostly intact, and the fauna to go with it. Because the conservationist Aldo Leopold had the foresight to advocate keeping the core of the place roadless from the 1920s on, it has been saved from irreversible fragmentation. Being human, and therefore blundering and arrogant, we've done our best to sully it, but certain crucial restraints have thwarted us. Leopold came to believe in the necessity of restraint after an early career filled with mistakes. He helped exterminate Mexican gray wolves, erroneous in his belief that a lack of predators would be good for deer; he believed in fire suppression and "getting out the cut." He later found his way out of the traps of conventional thinking—all the bad ideas he'd imbibed in a Yale education—and saw the world whole, as an infinite web of interlocking relationships: grass filtering runoff into rivers, rivers offering refuge to beavers, beavers slowing the flow of those rivers and creating marshlands beloved by elk, elk chased by Mexican gray wolves, wolves thus ensuring more evenly distributed grazing of grass by keeping the elk moving, and grass at the center of a thousand other relationships: grass and its companion, fire.

It remained possible, when I wrote those words, to hope we might maintain a significant swath of our old-growth conifer forest for decades to come in the Gila. Now most of it is but a memory, charred in the blink of an eye in megafires we didn't see coming. First the Whitewater-Baldy Fire, biggest in recorded state history, more than five hundred square miles, which roared over the Mogollon Mountains in 2012. Then the Silver Fire, more than two hundred square miles, which torched the Black Range and burned this peak in 2013.

the mountain knows the mountain

These fires changed the high country beyond recognition for those of us who knew it well. It is no longer deep green year-round, as so much of the new vegetation—aspen, oak, and locust—drops its leaves over the winter, making the country appear rather drab half the year. That may be part of why early spring is such an emotional struggle for me here, the absence of a green forest. But there is new grass everywhere.

> all the hip people
> agree that nature is doomed
> meanwhile the hawk hunts

I must continually remind myself that the concept of wilderness with a capital W—wild land managed by humans to keep at bay our most destructive tools and ensure we are visitors who do not remain—could only have emerged as a rearguard action from within a culture bent on destroying it.

> I will never know
> the mountain the way
> the mountain knows me,

april

moods bared like
my bottom
on the day of my birth:
sadness
at monsoon rains,
ecstasy
in lightning's burst,
skulking
dusklight search for bears,
a slab of meat eager
to excite its own blood;
but I know the spring
on the north face
where the mountain weeps
sweet tears of joy
at the coming of summer,
snowmelt filtered
through the roots
of grasses and forbs
and tender young aspens,
tickled on its trickle
through earth,
flavor clean as laughter,
mouthfeel that of mirth,
though I'm told
I anthropomorphize,
for whatever that's worth.

may

The scream of a hawk in the calm of the morning: I feel a visceral thrill at the sound, a tingle in the blood, and when the hawk moves on or goes silent, I feel unsettled by the quiet. Something in the sound speaks to me in a way beyond language or music, but I wade through the silence afterward seeking language or music, the sounds my ear knows. I turn on the FM radio and listen to the news. The news, as usual, is bad. I'm reminded I can do without it, indeed can do nothing about it. The hawk, though: the hawk had news of its own, if only I could tune in to the frequency.

demagogues babble
with missiles aimed & ready
vulture sits & waits

the house wrens trilling
six hundred songs an hour
like half-ounce coltranes

the mountain knows the mountain

When I first came to the mountain, I walked for hours in the days' last light. I covered miles. I went as far as I could to still return to the cabin by dark. I wanted to know the surrounding country, wanted to map for myself the broader neighborhood: who was eating what and where, how the water sheds at the pinnacle of the watershed. (Living at the top of the watershed means every which way you turn, the land sheds water.) It was a surrender to seduction to see where the trails led. My boots deepened the grooves in those trails, and the beauty along those trails carved new grooves in me. A path in the woods, I learned, was not just a way through but a way in: to the splendors of the country and the secrets of my own mind.

> lone spruce tree   north slope
> far from the rest of your kind
> i feel you brother

My friend and former fellow member of the lookout tribe Mark Johnson paid an afternoon visit in possession of a step counter (and tequila, and cigars, bless his heart). It showed that 13,300 steps were required for him to reach the mountain from the pass. With my slightly longer legs, I figure a reasonable estimate for

my own journey would be 12,500 steps, or 25,000 per round trip. In an average year, working ten days on and four days off, plus visiting now and again in the offseason, I make about twenty round trips, or half a million steps. Multiply that by the number of years I've worked here, and we're starting to get somewhere. Millions of steps along the same stretch of trail, familiar but never dull. Only now, in fact, am I truly beginning to know it, as I near eight million steps along its length.

> what an odd commute
> narrow path to a high place
> then climb into sky

At ten thousand feet above sea level, where the air starts to get thin, worldly ambition goes into cardiac arrest. The heart of striving gives out. All that's left of aspiration is to sing a song as brief and gorgeous as that of the Say's phoebe who lurks around the tower and the cabin every morning. And so I try once more to sing that song:

> fallen douglas fir
> i admired you while you stood
> now you heat my hut

may

    say's phoebe perches
  on the cabin's lightning rod
     a lookout comrade

Each year when I report for duty, I spend an hour or so in the district office. I sign paperwork and check out supplies: binoculars, two-way radios, weather implements. On one such occasion, I discovered a trove of photographs lying faceup in a trash can. I stuck my arm in the bin and retrieved one I recognized as having been part of a display of Forest Service history in the office foyer. The foyer having undergone redesign, the display was removed and casually tossed out like so much garbage: a perfect metaphor for the agency's relationship to its own past.

    When I inquired of my supervisor whether I might salvage a photo or two for myself, I was greeted with incredulity, as though I were a dumpster-diving hobo requesting permission to subsist on spoiled food. I took two of the photos, both of historic lookouts, feeling a little sheepish for some reason.

    Now I wish I'd kept them all.

      cat tracks in the snow
  night movements on the north slope
     mark of the hunter

the mountain knows the mountain

Although I wish it weren't so for what it implies of the human project, the presence of so much beauty here is dependent, to a large degree, on what is absent. A partial list would include no pavement, no stoplights, no litter, no sirens, no train whistles, no light pollution, no barking dogs, no pet cats killing songbirds, no television, no internet, no computers, no humans preening or pulling rank, no junk mail, no cops, no guns, no Border Patrol checkpoints, no billboards, no political yard signs, no neon, no fast food, no toxic masculinity (except my own), no domestic violence (except among the deer), no Jehovah's Witnesses knocking on the door, no visits from fascists—fascists don't hike anymore, turns out.

> hermit thrush singing
> makes me wonder if hermits
> always sing sweetest

> workplace safety sign
> close trap door on entering
> don't see that one much

> no way out but down
> this seven by seven room
> ain't for claustrophobes

may

Swallows dart and veer in mirrored pairs, inscribing their choreography on the sky framed by the tower windows. I close my eyes and see them again in my mind, their play a kind of admonition: do not squander your life in needless angst, fool!

> salami sandwich
> mustard   mayo   lettuce   cheese
> such banal daydreams

> just another fool
> gazing at the moon's mountains
> from an earth mountain

Simple chores take on spiritual significance. Dipping water from the cistern. Refreshing the hummingbird feeders with simple syrup. Setting the teapot in the afternoon sun to warm water for dishwashing. Swirling dirty clothes in the five-gallon pail I've marked LAUNDRY—in contrast to the one marked MOP—and hanging them on the line to dry. Building a fire in the wood stove to heat the cabin before bed. Half of what I think of as my spiritual life is comprised of such gestures, repeated daily. You cannot spell spiritual without ritual.

I recall Bill Murray's character in the movie *Groundhog Day* reliving the same day over and over until he got it right.

And what was that character's name? Yes. Phil Connors.

>glassing distant hills
>cutting wood   hauling water
>upkeep for the soul

I am walking most evenings in the footsteps of bears. Their sign is everywhere: to the north on the scalloped ridge line along the divide, back toward the pass on the crest trail, down around the pond on the flank of the ridge. Large, deep paw prints: big, healthy bears. They love what's growing back in the burn scar, the grasses and forbs, the berry bushes, the oaks laden with acorns. One of these days our paths will intersect in time and space, as happens every summer. Usually I am startled by the bear running away after it hears or smells me, and I am lucky to glimpse a dark blur bounding downslope. But every so often I see one before it knows I'm there, and I savor the moment of respect and humility I'm granted as I observe an animal more powerful than I am. This is their neighborhood, and they are its rulers; I am just a seasonal visitor.

may

You wish your smell did not incite fear
in the *osos*. You like to get oh so close

and watch, but you dream no harm,
want only to take a photograph,

not a skull, not a hide, not a trophy,
not a life. One wild moment in the presence

of a creature who could eat you
does a body righteous. Stay alert,

the body demands; stay humble,
the body whispers. Know, bodily, your place

in the food chain. Exercise your right to remain
silent in awe. Let go the need for a photo.

I would be pleased to know what the ancient ones, the Indigenous people, called this hump of rock, which their leavings indicate they regarded as sacred. This week I found the largest potsherd I've ever turned up here, as well as a piece of white stone worked like jewelry, with lines etched into its edges and a hole bored through its middle by some kind of tapered awl—a bead, I believe they call it out West. Strange and striking and just lying there in the dirt for the last thousand years, give or take. Finding it evoked similar feelings to seeing a bear. It was a reminder of my transience here, even as it connected me to the long, rich life of the place. It gives and gives, this mountain, and I merely want to be a worthy recipient of all it offers. Not a philosopher, a neo-Thoreauvian, a blinkered spelunker in the caverns of the self—but an eyeball. The most sensitive and discerning eyeball. Mary Oliver again: "Attention without feeling . . . is only a report."

> the elusive goal
> becoming pure eyeball mind
> minus an ego

Tonight I stepped outside for one last leak before bed, and right in the cone of light from my headlamp stood a fox, not ten yards away. We froze and stared at each other, my headlamp glowing a glacial blue in its eyes. After a slight cock of its head that made my soul feel seen, the fox turned and ran, its bushy tail swaying like a tiny dancer as it picked its way over the edge of the mountain and into the night. And later:

may

    ruckus in the dark
  wheelbarrow tipped on its side
    bear probing weakness

Standing on the top landing of the tower, looking off toward the Rio Grande—which ought to be renamed the Rio Dolor, or maybe the Rio Seco—I found myself face to face with a hummingbird that either confused me with a very large flower or found me curious and chose a closer look. Its brilliant red throat gorget flexed and glowed. "Hello, little friend," I said, and it turned and flew away.

Perhaps it knows who feeds it and wanted to say thanks.

    the hummingbirds dig
  the guy with the open bar
    dangling on his porch

My friend Jean visited today on a weekend off from her own fire tower, a recreational hike. She brought a bag of salt and vinegar chips, a Snickers bar, some gouda cheese, two oranges, and a package of Fig Newtons—like Santa Claus, if Santa were lean, tan, and female. My lady lookout friends are the best a man could ask for, the best there ever was in this line of work. All of them having started before me, they taught me how to do it by example. Jean sees not one artificial light from her tower, a source of envy among the rest of us. Rázik is going on twenty-seven years and Sara thirty-six on the mother mountain, a twelve-mile walk from the nearest road. My heroes! My friends and role models. Bless their beautiful, funky, flinty yet magnanimous souls.

> i know a lookout
> who breakdances when she's bored
> but i won't say who

It is strange and a little miraculous to be a fire lookout in the twenty-first century. Some days it feels almost illicit, sitting here getting paid to look out the window. We really ought to have been retired by now in a culture as omnivorous and remorseless as ours. *Isn't there an app for that*, I can hear the incredulous voice say, *a satellite, a super-duper camera, something?* Just be patient. In due time the technofetishists will usher us into obsolescence. As Randall Jarrell said, "Our culture is essentially periodical: we believe that all that is deserves to perish and to have something else put in its place." Give us just a few more years gawking at cloud shapes, communing with birds. Wait: maybe another decade or two, until all that remains of the post-Pleistocene forests has burned in the western United States. Then the gizmos of the futurists can have at it, and the last of us can be wheeled into a home for aged and infirm lookouts, where we can swap stories of the olden days before the last of the American wildlands were completely rationalized under the gaze of a cold, impassive, all-seeing eye; before every juicy black-bear fart was picked up by a giant parabolic microphone in the sky, cross-checked with a heat-sensitive satellite, attached to a GPS coordinate, and logged in a database of suspected four-legged terrorists.

> fifteen seasons in
> wondering what will doom me
> my knees or a drone

Lost causes, anachronisms: the defining motifs of my life. Born to a small family farm just before the death of the small family farm. Student and practitioner of print journalism just before the demise of print journalism. Writer of books at a time when attention spans are etched in the acid bath of the doom scroll. Fire lookout. I try to imagine what could possibly come next. Taxi driver? Typewriter repairman?

the mountain knows the mountain

from its haughty perch
nutcracker seems to jeer me
somehow that cheers me

a spider rappels
from the roof of the tower
eye on the deer fly

hey   short-horned lizard
pink as the rock you crouch on
almost stepped on you

Aspens killed by wildfire look like silver whiskers on the face of the mountains, as if fire were a razor that missed a spot.

hermit thrush singing
so sweetly from its treetop
hello to the day

may

Two deer move across the peak, along the edge of the meadow. Some sound spooks them; they turn and retrace their route, disappear into the trees. Ghost deer: there one minute, gone the next.

    hermit thrush singing
so sweetly from its treetop
    goodbye to the day

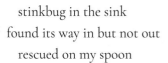

   stinkbug in the sink
found its way in but not out
   rescued on my spoon

   planning a caper
the fly on the countertop
   rubs its little hands

  mouse in the wood pile
thinks it was built just for her
    & maybe it was

I once met two women at a potter's studio near White Oaks, New Mexico. While I surveyed the wares for sale, the potter, Ivy, sat at her wheel. Her friend whose name I don't remember sat at an adjacent table working on an intricate clay mask. I remember Ivy's name because it's written into the back of the beautiful plates I bought that day, their black glaze inspired by a forest fire that had recently burned near White Oaks, so close that the char on the trees could be seen through the studio window. When I told the two of them, in response to their questions, that I spent summers as a lookout—in fact had come there on my days off the tower, on a weekend road trip—the potter's friend looked up from her mask and said: "I was once a lookout in Alaska, many years ago. Beautiful world it was up there. Some of the fires were huge and went on for weeks. I knew men who were paid by the Forest Service to stand beyond the edge of the fires and shoot burning deer and bears when they ran from the flames. If they weren't killed on the spot, the animals might run for half a mile or more, starting new spot fires ahead of the main smoke before they collapsed."

I have never forgotten that. Was she joshing me, thinking I looked like the credulous kind? It's the sort of story you don't know whether to believe, even as you refuse to fact-check it, aware you might be disappointed if it isn't true. The allure of insider knowledge—especially when colored with death.

> sit beneath the pines
> touch their sap   savor the scent
> you won't be here long

may

When a lookout gets a little over-introspective, high fire danger—and we are now well and truly into it—can feel like some weird blessing, demanding the snap into the here and now that others get rock-climbing or whitewater rafting. For me it's a cranking up on the dial of eyeball mind, that enchanted ocular stupor where you're caressing with your eyes a known landscape like a lover, every sensuous curve and ripple, including its scars—open-pit mines—all of them dotted with signposts of meaning and layered with a palimpsest of stories that fade with the urgency of detecting the anomaly, the sudden rupture that is a wisp of smoke. It took me a long time to understand that actively looking for smoke through binoculars is a fool's errand. Given the expansiveness of the view, I can see a single tree on fire at a distance of twenty-five miles with the naked eye. Smoke announces itself, no need to hunt for it. Just stay awake, stay alert.

Days like these, gusts to forty miles per hour, reacquaint me with the sense of responsibility attaching to the work—and its weird joys. Among them: turning my face into the gale from the top landing of the tower and feeling my cheeks ripple like the surface of a pond when a frog jumps in. Or spending six straight hours slowly turning circles in surveillance of a piece of the Earth to make a person weep at its beauty and cruelty. I did not understand, in the beginning, how necessary was the cruelty to the allure of the place. That feature was crucial in order for it to mirror the human world, except for the fact that the land's cruelty harbors no actual malice. It just is: a function of severe topography and searing aridity.

I see here an example of one of the problems of writing for me. So often it comes out wrong the first time. I look back at my description of watching over the landscape two paragraphs ago and am filled with disgust by its imprecision. As if flummoxed by the difficulty of explaining my complex relationship with this piece of country, I lean on the worn old crutch of cliché: the lover. Embedded in that metaphor, for a man, is the assumption of an objectifying gaze and a certain arrogant possessiveness. But it is simply not the case that I can claim possession of this landscape, nor can I assume it responds to me the way a lover might. It is closer to the truth to admit that I am possessed by it, that I respond to *it* the way a lover might. Recently I came across reference to something once said by Cézanne: "The landscape thinks itself in me, and I am its consciousness." That feels more accurate, situating the agency within the landscape, not with me—by making me the vessel for the landscape's expression of itself.

More accurate—but maybe not entirely so. Just as often, I feel the landscape's total indifference to me and my existence. This can be unnerving but also liberating. By planting myself inside a place that regards me as nothing, regards me not at all, I am reoriented to my true importance in the scheme of things, which is nil. Therein lies an invitation to freedom. If I am nothing, I can make anything of my life I wish.

may

the landscape beckons
hinting at oblivion
the raven just laughs

When the Big Sad moves in, I take the trail no one knows to the
place no one goes. Not even melancholy can follow me there.

fifty days on lookout
and not a single smoke
some years roll like that
an extravagant indolence
paid to sit watch and wait
for a thing that keeps not
keeps   not   happening
until you start to hope it
never does: your hours
of uneventful vigilance
appearing in retrospect
like performance art
performed for no one

june

Moon waxing, the cabin is owned by the miller moths at night. They strain against the glass seeking release toward the light. Dozens at first, then hundreds—impossible to count them as they move incessantly with a low hum, like static. All I can do is prepare for bed early and keep the lights off after dark.

bark torn from the pines
claw marks in the cambium
bears dining on moths

the mountain knows the mountain

June 3, another anniversary: that of the Gila Wilderness (1924), and that of my brother's suicide (1996). I've always found it peculiar, and somehow meaningful, that the declaration of the wilderness (the first in human history) and the end of Dan's life (my one and only brother) happened on the same calendar day. It's as if the fates prearranged a place of consolation for the most violent rupture in my life, and tipped me to the linkage with that shared date. This is the natural temptation, no? Take a coincidence and make something more of it, something extraterrestrial, when in fact it is precisely terrestrial: rooted in the land and my relation to the land, which is the thing that makes the coincidence beautiful, the convergence meaningful. Every year on this day, I feel grateful beyond words to have found the Gila. It was my search for some remnant of Dan that first brought me within reach of it, his death in New Mexico responsible for my introduction to, and eventual obsession with, this landscape—its clarity and brutality, its rude beauty. All suggestive of him, it occurs to me: the ruthless clarity of his renunciation of life. The brutality of the gunshot. The beauty that was his final and enduring gift to me, hot-air ballooning together above Albuquerque, back in 1995, when he gave me my first real taste of sky the last time I saw him alive. This wilderness offered a solitude to match my loneliness, and the mountain lent my loneliness a measure of dignity by giving me another flavor of sky on a scale I'd never known. Would I have survived my grief if I hadn't found this place? Maybe. Maybe. I've been dying of beauty since the day I showed up here, but "a little dying never killed anyone," as my friend Ben Saenz, that brilliant and sensitive soul, says in one of his poems. The long life of these mountains humbles me. I bow before their majesty. I exalt in insignificance.

june

    bug flew in my ear
intent on casing the joint
    not a whole lot there

    sun-shower bladder
strung from a hook on the porch
    above two white moons

    hanging from the line
underwear   a pair of pants
    and a butterfly

Trails of virga dangle like jellyfish tentacles from the bellies of the cumulus clouds. Another day of eyeballing sky: tough duty, but someone's gotta make the fourteen bucks an hour. May as well be a curmudgeonly depressive better left out of social circulation for the sake of social cohesion.

    missing ice cream   wine
mushroom & onion pizza
    but not all that much

    two months on the peak
hiking every evening
    no more beer belly

the mountain knows the mountain

Two new fires yesterday, one of which I spotted, a few miles east of Signal Peak. Fifteen years of this work, and more than a hundred fires called in—I barely bother to mention them in my notebooks anymore, they've become so routine—but still a little of the old thrill persists, especially those first moments when you know you hold a secret as the only human in the world who sees the smoke. The latest: the Bear Fire, named for Bear Canyon. *El Fuego del Oso.* It shows no sign of wanting to get big. Maybe it is destined to remain a cub.

> smoke in the distance
> a moth trapped in the tower
> unperturbed by fire

Water has collected in tiny tinajas all over the mountain from last night's rain. One of them sits adjacent to the tower. I spend part of this afternoon watching Steller's jays and dark-eyed juncos give themselves baths in it. They look funny when they're finished, their feathers all fluffed, an avian version of bed head.

The mountain offers many gifts, among them visions of avian bed head, but it also ruins a person for any sort of work other than sitting on it watching.

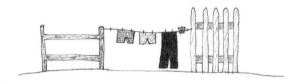

the mountain knows the mountain

> from dawn until dusk
> looking at these arid peaks
> awaiting the spark

"Why the sudden turn to haiku?" my friend Mark Ehling asked in a letter recently. A good question, and one I keenly wanted to answer, as no other friend has been so central to my creative life—our conversations and correspondence about reading and writing ongoing now for twenty-five years. He was there for my fledgling undergraduate efforts, and his encouragement dragged me out of more than one creative morass in later years. Haiku has certainly marked a swerve in my writing life, away from works of narrative nonfiction—storytelling sustained to a length of 75,000 words—toward radical compression. As I thought about an answer, I remembered it was another friend's intervention that proved crucial. In the midst of convalescing from my hip surgeries, I told my friend Nina MacLaughlin that a year of chronic pain had destroyed my ability to read. I couldn't finish a book. She promptly sent me an anthology of Bashō, Buson, and Issa. If I couldn't read a book, maybe I could begin with three lines of poetry. Her kindness coaxed me out of my funk; that book is among the sweetest gifts anyone ever gave me.

june

Writing my own haiku, I discovered, was a way to continue playing with language in the absence of a larger project. Inspiration often finds a foothold in imitation. The brevity of the form turned out to be not a constraint but a liberation. It allowed me to say certain things I couldn't have said any other way. The three Japanese masters, as I read and reread them, sounded as though they were talking across the centuries straight to me. Even more profound: they had lived versions of my life, long before I ever showed up.

Matsuo Bashō:

How admirable!
to see lightning and not think
    life is fleeting.

Yosa Buson:

My arm for a pillow,
I really like myself
    under the hazy moon.

Kobayashi Issa:

Napped half the day;
no one
    punished me!

Modern practitioners of English haiku generally scorn the 5-7-5 rule, regarding it as stilted and opposed to spontaneity, overly wordy—fine for a soundbite, not for a poem. They point to grammatical differences between English syllables and Japanese sound units as a reason to be free of it. Other laws have hardened. To survey the critical commentary on modern English haiku is to be besieged by orthodoxies. A haiku must contain two different images. It must not employ rhyme. It must not be composed of a single sentence. It must eschew the personal, avoid ideas, never generalize, never use a simile, and never reference the past or the future, only the present. It must stand alone, not gesturing to any poem before or after. It must involve nature, but not human nature, because humans, it is implied, are divorced from nature. As with many specialized forms of artistic practice, elaborate battlements are always being erected by the self-appointed forces of customs and border protection. Aware the art in English is necessarily impure—for how could authentic haiku be written in a language not Japanese?—they compensate by imposing rigorous new standards of purity.

This dishonors the complex history of haiku. The form originated in the three-line, seventeen-syllable *hokko* that marked the start of a series of linked verses known as *renga*. Renga was typically created by groups of poets in social settings under strict rules about seasonal references and how many times blossoms and the moon must appear. Haiku as a discrete form emerged when hokku broke free from the rigorous structure of renga, and from renga's communal nature. Strange, then, that we should wish to

june

put it back in a cage. Stranger still that I would think to consult the critics when learning to write haiku, which is like reading *Rolling Stone* to learn how to sing a song. Haiku's first masters would be denigrated as hooligans by today's standards. The three poems above would be thrown on the reject pile of any modern haiku contest. They sound too contemporary. They violate the injunction to keep haiku impersonal and objective. They make poetry from the movement of a specific consciousness. Worse, they do it with a sense of humor, a sly irony. Consider Issa once more, from his great haibun *The Spring of My Life*:

> pretending wisdom,
> a man tells a woman all
> about the eclipse

Has the concept of mansplaining ever been more skillfully rendered—and in fewer words—than in this poem from two centuries ago, which is one self-contained sentence, says nothing about nature, and violates so many other rules of haiku?

Reading the critical guardians of English haiku made me want to write a longer poem for the first time in my life. Their dos and don'ts inspired the effort, written as a gift to my friend Bobby Byrd on his birthday this April. It helps to know that Bobby is a poet of some renown, three decades my senior, which makes my instructing him in how to write a poem by writing a bit of doggerel (called, naturally, "How to Write a Poem") doubly absurd, or maybe triply so. Thank goodness he has a sense of humor.

the mountain knows the mountain

It has to in some way be metaphorical.
It should make you sound like some meta-oracle.
Split your infinitives to show you don't care.
Make them look here when the meaning is there.

If your poem mentions birds, throw it away.
If your poem has swords, make them sashay.
How to renounce iambic pentameter?
Dance a jig while waving a bent scimitar.

Avoid, if you can, needless repetition.
Deploy, if you're wan, heedless superstition.
Whatever you do, do not make it rhyme.
This makes you sound like you're not of your time.

Despite what they say, don't write what you know.
Try always to tell and never to show.
When your poem wins a prize, mime being humble.
Write your speech out to ensure you don't mumble.

If the muse disappears, pop pseudoephedrine.
If the news brings you tears, try judo or good gin.
Whatever you do, do not make a joke.
Your license to practice may be revoked.

Most crucial of all, avoid having fun.
A poem made right should bark like a gun.
Your concealed carry permit means the meaning is coded.
Your thumb on the safety means the diction is loaded.

june

I took to the 5-7-5 rule in haiku because I enjoy seeing what's possible within the vessel of a fixed form. It may be that a fixed form is especially attractive in a place where the days and weeks can be so formless. As Liz Lerman put it, "Think inside the box." That could be my job description. I work inside a steel and glass box, where I spend all day thinking. Plus I live in area code 575. How can I not embrace the omen? Conforming to a syllable count may be the unsophisticated way of writing haiku, but I'm trying my damndest to remain unsophisticated here, in all ways and manners, so as to stay open to astonishment and undefended against beauty.

I mingle features of haiku with some of *senryu*, which in Japanese follows the same 5-7-5 form in three lines, but treats matters of the human realm with a comic, satiric, or sardonic intelligence. Beyond that, I have no plan. I don't strive for greatness, don't dream of glory. It's been noted that Issa wrote twenty thousand haiku, most of them bad; I revere his example. Most of mine are bad too. I reject notions of holy purity and am left cold by the strain of English haiku that aims to sound as if written in what the poet imagines to be the hushed and rapturous voice of the year 1679. Better Gary Snyder's conception of the form, as practiced by non-Japanese poets: "fresh, new, experimental, youthful and playful, unpretentious, and available to students and beginners who want to try out a poetic way of speaking." To maintain spontaneity and silliness, I try not to think of my poems as haiku at all, or even senryu, but rather as a scraggly, bastardized cousin I jokingly call *lowku*, bad pun intended. Another way to say it is that I write three-line, seventeen-syllable prose poems, hoping to remain a beginner, playful and unpretentious. If writing long prose narratives feels like going to work wearing clothes, then writing short poems is akin to playing around naked. What freedom! Capital letters, punctuation: away with you, all you unnecessary baubles . . .

I once decided I wanted a writing career that moved in stages toward a vanishing act. Begin by publishing a book with one of the big corporate houses in New York. Then another with a mid-sized firm, a third with a mom-and-pop indie, a fourth with a university press, followed by a self-published, limited edition, and end by scratching haiku in the skin of aspen trees miles from the nearest road, in a place known only to bears. Move always toward a deepening obscurity.

I am more than halfway there.

> poems carved in bark
> soft words made for vanishing
> scored by the bear's claw

Some of my poems are first and foremost keepsakes from moments of pure noticing. One evening I sat in the tower, reading a book, when I heard a raven cry. I put the book down and moved to the open, north-facing window—and just then a zone-tailed hawk flew by at eye level. I picked up my pen and wrote three lines in as brief a time as it took to notice the moment they commemorated:

> cry of the raven
> in the calm of the evening
> zone-tailed hawk floats past

june

It was the writing of the words that helped me understand these two things were connected, one a response to the other.

Other times it's a matter of wrestling with a spontaneous thought or image by finessing the phrasing, working through five or fifteen versions before landing on the one that feels right. I wrote at least a dozen drafts to arrive on this one:

> lost in the mountains
> move as if you were water
> you shall soon be found

This was a piece of wisdom given me by a skilled outdoorsman of the Gila Wilderness. Ian the Kid, his friends called him, for his slight resemblance to Billy the Kid. I had asked him a simple question. If you got lost in the woods, what would you do? I kept trying to start the poem—

> i asked a man once
> what to do when lost outdoors

—and it kept not working. I realized that the form is just too compressed to accommodate a dialogue. I needed to transform a Q&A into an aphorism, even if the haiku priesthood typically views aphorisms as unpoetic: too much telling, not enough showing. Ian the Kid had given me a wise and useful answer: pretend you are water, succumb to gravity, find your way to the valleys. Perhaps there was no terrible larceny involved in making it mine. Indeed, if ever asked the same question, I would offer the same answer.

the mountain knows the mountain

By sharing his wisdom, he enlarged mine. He wasn't the sort to demand attribution in a footnote.

Sometimes I take a charged event, a shock, a tragedy, and corral it within the form while enhancing some of its mystery:

> neither man nor horse
> returned from their sunset ride
> vultures dined for weeks

This was written after my friend John's death near his fire tower, an evening horseback accident during which both horse and rider perished in a fall. I wrote tens of thousands of words about him, about our friendship and what his death meant to me—he became the major character in a book—but even after all of that, he started showing up in my poems. Maybe I wanted to make the story of his death as mythical as it felt in the moment, and prose just wasn't up to the task. Whatever the reason, I wasn't done with him. Certain inferences in the poem were untethered from facts on the ground, although I don't think John would have minded, with his mischievous and irreverent personality. He did not become sustenance for vultures. His body was promptly removed upon discovery by search and rescue. But the horse that fell dead on top of him was left where the two of them dropped, and over the course of a couple of weeks, Sundance's carcass was picked clean. Something macabre in me likes the spooky implication of "vultures dined for weeks." There's just no room to distinguish that they dined only on horseflesh.

june

No other creature has been such a continuous presence at the fire lookout. Their gliding, circling flight around the tower has a way of reminding a man that he is destined to cease eating and be eaten—someday, some way, maybe by a feathered forager, maybe by a worm. In teaching you that you are minuscule in the scheme of things here on the fecund Earth, the job also fosters a feeling of singularity. Who else in their daily work receives the gift of such a profound lesson? In reminding you that you are not special—over and over, every day—the mountain paradoxically makes you feel special for being the recipient of a message so few heed in a time of preening self-branding and limitless self-exposure. Imagining yourself an apostle of the message, you find you're seized by delusions of grandeur—a preening prophet after all—à la Kerouac and his famous stint on Desolation Peak up in the North Cascades, a mountain overrun now by tourists.

> pilgrims   offerings
> they are the fate of this peak
> just not till you die

Immediately I find the thought absurd, self-aggrandizing, unaccountably arrogant—this mountain crawling with gawkers seeking contact with the ghost of the man who gave it renown, in other words *me*—and I turn back to the silliness that sometimes inflects the experience here, as a way of poking holes in my outlandishly swollen pretensions.

the mountain knows the mountain

a fart with the wind
perchance a fart into it
depends on the mood

even on lookout
amorous forenoons go wrong
spoiled by day hikers

Ambiguity is one flavor of a short poem. Does the amorous forenoon involve one human or two?

To study the progression of haiku from Bashō through Buson and Issa, and on to Masaoka Shiki, the fourth of the great masters, is to understand that the form is supple and pliant, forever in the process of being reinvented. That reinvention continues to this day among the more interesting of the English haiku poets. Every rule ever made has been bent or broken by new poets trying new things. ("In every case be different," Buson advised, "advance without regard to whether you are being traditional or innovative.") Some haiku do tell stories. Some are vehicles for ideas. Some involve wordplay and rhyme. Many exhibit a pungent personality, and often the best—although I know others would disagree—are the funny ones.

I'm not the only person to have found the form a solace in the midst of illness. Richard Wright, the American writer best known for his novel *Native Son* and his memoir *Black Boy*, spent his last years writing more than four thousand haiku as his health slipped away in France. Shiki wrote many haiku while sick with tuberculosis. Bedbound, he made poetry from whatever was near at hand. I found, after writing my fart poem, that Shiki had written one too:

> Didn't burn incense
> didn't pass wind
> half a spring day

A poem in which the essential line wrings meaning from the absence of a fart, while insinuating, with one subtle word (half), that the absence did not last: How liberated I felt in reading it! It validated my own weird efforts, even though his poem of flatulence is more elegant than mine. Haiku poets, he wrote, "try to encompass every inch of the world." Imagine my delight when I discovered that he had written an essay offering a taxonomy of haiku about shit, piss, and outhouses.

According to translator Burton Watson, Shiki "believed bad poems as well as good should be recorded so that one could learn from one's mistakes." Experimentation is the name of the game. Failure is to be embraced and owned. Everyone rips stinky farts. Some are called to make poems of them. And so I record my mistakes and poeticize my farts, experiment and fail, try to learn from the failure, experiment some more and fail again, try to fail better, fail smarter, fail funnier, fail goofier. This notebook is littered with failures, almost every attempt to write haiku ending up an illustration of how not to write haiku. But I find it useful to look back on the precise path taken on the stumbling, bumbling journey toward that elusive state known as "haiku mind," which comes only intermittently for a mind like mine. I can get away with this because I'm doing it for myself, in private, not for an audience of so-called "followers" prepared, at the slightest perceived lapse, to savage my efforts. Were I practicing in public, in the forms and forums where most of us now write, I would have been hounded into silence by vicious trolls before I truly began: the greatest failure of all.

Instead I follow the path marked by Bashō:

> When the sun has begun to sink behind the rim of the hills, I
> sit quietly in the evening waiting for the moon so I may have
> a shadow for company, or light a lamp and discuss right and
> wrong with my silhouette ... I am not really the kind who is
> so completely enamored of solitude that he must hide every
> trace of himself away in the mountains and wilds. It's just
> that, troubled by frequent illness and weary with dealing with
> people, I've come to dislike society. Again and again I think of
> the mistakes I've made in my clumsiness over the course of the
> years ... I've worn out my body in journeys that are as aimless
> as the winds and clouds and expended my feelings on flowers
> and birds. But somehow I've been able to make a living this
> way, and so in the end, unskilled and talentless as I am, I give
> myself wholly to this one concern, poetry.

I could borrow every word but the very last to describe my life. I've given myself wholly not to poetry, but to the mountain.

june

    an entire week
  without any visitors
      this mountain redoubt

I've been using the sorriest sawhorse in the known history of sawhorses, and I finally tired of it. It still did the job. I cut a lot of firewood on it over the years. But it leaned drastically to one side and was sun-bleached a dead gray. It sent a message of decrepitude to all who glimpsed it. Its time for change had come. One afternoon of repair work plus a coat of stain, and I now own a sawhorse a person can be proud of. I find myself looking at it for the twentieth time and silently nodding my head: a job (modestly) well done. It still tilts slightly, a result of its repairman having only two hands, not four, and only one sawhorse at his disposal. It would have been nice to have two more to make a platform on which to rebuild this one. But if I had two more, I wouldn't need to rebuild this one . . .

Thus the mind spirals in the absence of the usual stimuli.

    the bite of the saw
  releases perfume of pine
      into evening air

A day of insects: ladybugs, flies, and thousands of little gray-winged black bugs whose name I do not know, but who seem to know mine. They crawl all over the tower, and occasionally into my nostrils and ears. The forest is smoked over from fires, and the air is hot and still. Color has drained from the sky. Every part of me sweats, most of all my feet. Far from the most pleasant conditions here, but there is no place I would rather be. If the apocalypse is nigh, as it would seem to be, I want a good view of it.

>   these old birkenstocks
>   more comfortable each year
>   and stinkier too

A dozen Clark's nutcrackers flew in around 6:30 p.m. like some aerial circus act, squawking and screaming. They landed on the top branches of a snag, hung out there for three minutes like they were casing the joint, then peeled away in pairs and threes. I marvel at their industriousness; they collect and hide tens of thousands of pine seeds across the landscape, making this mountain range their pantry by burying five or six seeds at a time in the dirt or caching them in trees. I sometimes watch for half an hour at a time through binoculars as one performs

a balance-beam routine, clinging to a limb, swinging its body with tremendous force, its beak acting on cone scales like the tip of a miner's pick. The bird's expandable pocket beneath the tongue can hold a hundred or more seeds at once, and its spatial memory allows it to recall thousands of hiding places as far as fifteen or twenty miles away from its favorite source trees. Among the seeds it fails to retrieve, some germinate, replicating the pine forest on which the birds rely. The Johnny Appleseeds of certain pine species in North America, they are a good part of what makes life on this mountain so lively, with their flashy black-and-white wings and vocal presence in the treetops. They are the local extroverts, impossible to miss and easy to love, though of course the introverts delight me too.

> awoke feeling sad
> listened to the hermit thrush
> & was sad no more

Having heard whispers of the idea, I judge it inevitable that someday, some bureaucrat—geeked on monetizing the backcountry experience and importing the values of commercial tourism into what remains of the New Mexico wilderness—will propose renting this lookout as a bed and breakfast. There will of course be a branding effort (Bear BnB?), and there will remain a job

june

here. While infrared cameras linked with pattern-recognition software perform the fire watch duties, the caretaker will make pancakes for the tourists, lead nature walks each afternoon, and perform a rousing chautauqua each night around the campfire while dressed as Smokey Bear.

Please, sky gods, do me a favor and let me be dead and gone by then.

> I try to write an ode to wind
> as the wind seethes in the pines
> but its song subsumes my song.
> I try to write a poem of sun
> as the sun does its thing in sky
> but the glare makes it come out wrong.
>
> Everything here goes about whatever
> is the opposite of what we call *business*.
> Each bird sings its song whenever
> the wind relents and lets it.
> The mule deer embody good posture and fitness.
> The gophers tunnel. The vultures tilt.
>
> My mind funnels. My vision wilts.
> Not knowing my purpose, I fear
> I lack the talent to lack one.
> Mascot for mountain tree frogs?
> Voyeur to kinky salamanders?
> I dream the moon peeks up my kilt.

Supply exceeds demand for nature poems.
The screen people do adore their telephones.
The wind turns shy, the sun ducks out,
the gophers slumber, the vultures roost,
and here at last my purpose deduced:
giving the notion of uselessness a boost.

This afternoon a turkey vulture surveyed the meadow, swooped low, and landed fifty feet west of the tower. It stood motionless for a moment. It began dipping its head slightly, as if bowing or sniffing the earth; it walked a small semicircle around an exposed rock; it bent and plucked a dead mouse from the grass. It held the morsel in its beak, then threw back its head and swallowed it whole. Twice it jerked its neck as if forcing the mouse down its throat. It surveyed the meadow for a moment more, then launched itself airborne, soaring away to the south.

    the vulture circles
  its shadow passes over
      the living shiver

june

Mónica arrived over the weekend, her first visit of the season. The place is instantly transformed from hermetic abode to honeymoon hideaway, the nights warmer, the birdsong more joyous. I feel fortunate to have married a woman who appreciates the beauty of this place and recognizes the value of my season of solitude, a woman who doesn't denigrate my life here as "little boy games," as did someone I once loved. To have one's vocation, one's center of meaning, judged childish: there is no forgetting such a thing. The tone of contempt that framed the words, which indicated this was more than mere teasing, hit me like a slap across the face, I will admit. But if growing into a man means forgoing play and divorcing oneself from intimacy with the nonhuman, I suppose I'd prefer to remain a little boy playing games. Alan Watts, the great interpreter of Zen Buddhism, put it well: "To play so as to be relaxed and refreshed for work is not to play, and no work is well and finely done unless it, too, is a form of play."

Still, I must carry the scar of a wound, else why so quickly pivot from celebration of my sweet amor's arrival to the memory of an old insult? It is the scourge of the neurotic to greet a moment of joy with bitter recall of its opposite. Surely a true Zen hermit would carry the baggage of a doomed romance—and all the misunderstandings thereof—like a pair of sheer silk underpants, the weight of it no more than a whisper. Unfortunately, I know too little of Zen and am only an amateur hermit, dream though I do of one day turning pro.

I suppose I need to remind myself how fortunate I am not to have a shadow cast over my time here by the person closest to me. It is a serious piece of liberation to feel the cloud of critical judgment pass over the horizon, replaced by the warm glow of understanding and encouragement. Better still: to deepen the attachment I feel to this place alongside a sympathetic intelligence, a woman with the patience to teach me once more how to love. A woman who brings chocolate!

> three months   no haircut
> starting to look like a man
> with real religion

Tonight we hiked the loop around the mountain, which Mónica assumed was nice, gentle, and easy. If I'd known she thought that, I'd have told her otherwise. The thorns on the locust tore at our pants. The light drained away in the west. The steep switchbacks at the end made our muscles burn and our lungs strain for air. And there, amid the mature aspens encircling the sloping meadow dotted with gooseberry bushes, we saw a bear. Cinnamon-colored, a loner, likely male, mature. It turned sideways to us, ambled a ways, stopped, took off at a brisker pace when we moved for a better view. Mónica's first bear sighting—something she had both desired and feared—and a calm one, as most here are, the bears inclined to shy away from humans, aware of what we represent.

june

Nonetheless, a special flavor of adrenaline: the sort that results from encounter with an animal that could eat you. What a treat to have given her that, minus the gnawing on appendages.

> the bear flashed its rump
> as it crashed off through the brush
> mooning the voyeurs

Overnight, smoke drifted across the divide and settled in the low country west of the Rio Grande. This morning the world that way looked like a lake beneath fog, mountains like little islands rising blue-gray through the smoke mist—a strange and spectral sight, perhaps not so different from the time, sixty million years ago, when the country wasn't country but a vast inland sea.

> morning moves slowly
> afternoon moves slower still
> at last there is night

the mountain knows the mountain

One odd feature of this job is the mixture of envy and contempt it arouses in my office-bound colleagues. The envy arises because we lookouts get to live alone in the forest several months a year, unencumbered by staff meetings, overbearing bosses, and piles of paperwork—the unholy triumvirate of annoyances for the desk jockey. The contempt arises, at least in part, from our pay grade: GS–04, near to lowest in an agency imbued with a sense of military-style hierarchy. But the contempt also serves a deeper purpose as a kind of compensatory measure against the envy. No one likes feeling envious of someone else. It's much more satisfying to pretend we despise a lifestyle we secretly covet.

All of which makes for some deeply weird interactions on the rare instances when I appear in the office. I remember many years of my boss asking me, as part of my annual performance review, what my plans were for advancement within the agency. I told him again and again that I had no plans for advancement within the agency. Why? It is axiomatic: The lower the pay grade, the more time you get in the woods; the higher you climb the Forest Service ladder, the less time you spend outdoors. Finally he stopped asking the question. Only a lookout would answer the way I had. It was a response that was incomprehensible to him. Who doesn't wish to advance from a temporary seasonal job that pays a pittance and offers no retirement benefits?

My colleagues speak a language—land-management bu-reaucratese—I refuse to understand, peppered as it is with acronyms and jargon that do violence to the beauty of the English language. But speaking it reinforces their sense of being part of an esoteric priesthood, opaque to outsiders, and I am

june

continually reminded I am one of the outsiders. My concerns are alien to them: the ever-changing contents of bear scat over the course of the summer, the prevalence of white-pine blister rust on the limber pines, the relative robustness of the miller moth population year to year. I suppose I am describing a classic case of mutual incomprehension between indoor people and outdoor people, the former at home with procedures and protocols, rules and clocks, the world as it appears on paper or on a screen; the latter drawn to the satisfactions of using the senses we are all given at birth, sniffing at the fecundity of the world, touching it with our hands, watching with amazement the richness of the life around us.

> unaware i'm there
> a cinnamon bear noses
>   through the meadow grass

I tend not to write much when Móni is on the mountain. Why write when I am happy just being? I am reminded how much writing and depression have always been linked for me—scribbling as the way out of darkness. The intimacy of it has often felt like a secret whispered to myself, a result, perhaps, of my creative life having taken place in solitude for so many years that I find it a challenge to write if I know another human is within five miles.

I have become, I reckon, the spelunker in the caverns of the self I proclaim not to want to be.

We've been cooking, baking cookies, taking evening walks, reading, talking about what we're reading, laughing at our private little word games, making love. My customary angst has dissipated, my preemptive mourning for things I haven't lost, my wackadoodle ego-tripping over things I desire that will never be mine. Enough with the nonsense. Back to essentials. Clouds. Sunset light. Lightning and fire. Lizards on the rocks. Steller's jays in the pines. The curve of a hip. The taste of a kiss. The bliss of all this: this mountain, this sky, this moment together on high.

lightning in the north
strobing gold against the clouds
the lookout giggles

july

The first salamander of the season peeked from its hole in the morning, the first rufous hummingbird of the season arrived at the feeder in the afternoon, a great horned owl visited the meadow at twilight—the day kept getting more abundant in its gifts, *more perfect*, as Norman Maclean might have put it.

Now we sit by the outdoor fire with a quarter moon overhead and lightning flashing in the distance to the east. A light northeast breeze promises storms tomorrow. But tomorrow feels a long way off. It is one of those days I think of as thick. Time slowed and became dense with incident and spectacle, from smoky-valleyed morning to sunset-hour rainbow, not to mention all the creatures we observed in between. I read Norman Maclean's *A River Runs Through It* in the tower, an annual ritual, while Mónica read a history of Exxon on the cot in the shade of a white pine, her nearness a source of comfort to me. "I am haunted by waters"—those five words always slay me, and naturally I want to plagiarize that perfect final sentence, with one minor change.

I am haunted by flames.

My companions: ravens, vultures, foxes, and bears.
My mentors: stars, clouds, lightning, and fires.

Or maybe I'm mixed up—my mentors, bears and vultures;
my companions, stars and fires, light above and below.

I have not always been a good student.
My attention has too often turned inward,

to the self and its pains, its hungers.
Shedding ego is harder than it sounds

even for a dedicated solitary.
But each day offers a new chance

to relearn the timeless things,
bears scratching their muddy backs on trees,

vultures going about their recycling,
owls gliding under a waxing moon.

Mónica's account of the day being much better and more thorough, I feel obliged to share an excerpt from her journal, with her permission.

july

Today began with a salamander and ended with an owl. To describe this day, Felipe quoted from *A River Runs Through It*. Days like today, he said, keep getting "more perfect." Just when you think the mountain has given you enough, it goes and gives you just a little more. Just when you feel content with what you've seen and experienced, the mountain throws one more wonderful thing at you. That's what the owl was for me tonight.

On my last ten-day hitch here, it was the glowing pair of fox eyes in the meadow beside the cabin—that after an incredible bear encounter, only my second on the mountain. Two hours before that encounter, I was peeking down the north slope from the edge of the mountaintop when I heard a sound like big tree branches breaking apart. It was a heavy sound, and I thought immediately of a bear. I walked down just a few paces, peered into the trees, and after a few moments I could see a dark shape moving in the distance. I couldn't really tell what it was, but at one point I thought I saw a snout. I debated with myself about moving forward to investigate but ultimately decided against it. I'd had my first bear encounter only two evenings before—and while it was a peaceful encounter, I still didn't feel confident enough to be alone in close proximity to a bear. So I walked back to the safety of the mountaintop and the cabin.

When Felipe came down off the tower, I told him about what I had heard and saw, and we resolved to go down and look for bear sign once he was out of service. I couldn't shake the feeling that there was something down there. At quitting time we both pulled long-sleeved shirts over our heads and looked at each other before stepping out the door. "Let's go look for *osos, bebecita*," Felipe said with a grin and a twinkle in his eyes.

He saw the bear first. He stopped and a put a finger to his lips, then pointed. A beautiful young cinnamon bear, almost golden in color, was poking under rocks on the far side of a meadow. We tiptoed behind it for ten or fifteen minutes, silently watching it amble along and turn over stones looking for grubs. Once it even tipped over a rock and startled itself, jumping backwards. I never thought I would get to spend so much time in the presence of a bear, just watching it go about its life in the wild. And then, a few hours later, the glowing fox eyes . . . More perfect! It's all so much, I can't even write it all down, and I'm telling the stories all out of order.

Today is day six of our second ten-day hitch together, and I am officially "in the groove," as Felipe says. "Getting in the groove" is the phrase he uses to describe the moment when you're finally in sync with the rhythms of the mountain after arriving here from some other place, particularly a city. It's when your senses finally and fully experience the magic of this place, and it's usually accompanied by feelings of never wanting to leave or, in my case, of hoping to return quickly next year after a nine-month graduate-degree program in New York City. I didn't expect to feel this way about this place. I certainly thought I would enjoy it, but this deep sense of awe, this desire to draw it all in, inhale it deeply like taking in some vital (primordial?) liquid I have long been denied and didn't even know I needed: wow, this I did not anticipate.

july

And it goes without saying that I love it. I'm so grateful to be experiencing it. Heck, so many of us civilized bipeds—walking and driving through cities, running the hamster wheel of job, family, day-to-day problems, bigger and longer-term problems—need this. It is more than a vacation, much more than simply an escape. I don't quite know how to describe it. It's been nearly eight months since I left my job, and I haven't missed it for a second. I haven't even felt strange or out of place or uncomfortable being unemployed. On the contrary, it's felt totally natural, necessary even. I'm so thankful for the luxury of being able to do it. I may have less than $4,000 to my name, which is a little scary, but barring any major unexpected expense, I think I'm going to make it. Come early September I'll start to receive my scholarship money, and I'll begin my new, temporary life in New York. For now I am here on this glorious mountaintop, and I can hardly believe my good fortune.

But I need to go back to the beginning of this day. It started with my waking up in the early morning hours, when it was still dark, to see a spooky, orangey-yellow half moon just above the horizon, about level with the dark, shadowy outlines of pine trees in the meadow. Up here, unlike in the city, you become intimate with the phases and movements of celestial bodies like the moon. The sky was an eerie, grayish, almost purple color, and the wildfire smoke in the air hid the few town lights I would have otherwise seen in the distance. It was a beautiful, exhilarating sight. I even saw the dark outline of a deer grazing just outside the cabin window.

the mountain knows the mountain

After breakfast I discovered a new creature when I went out to pee beside the cabin. Squatting over the grass, I saw two dark eyes on either side of an oval-shaped face peering out from a hole in the ground. At first I thought it might be a vole, but I quickly realized it wasn't. It was a salamander! It had a serene, almost friendly face, and it stayed motionless, poking out of its hole. I found an injured grasshopper to toss its way, and it very slowly inched its way out of its hole to take a bite. I captured the moment in slow motion on my camera. You could watch as the salamander opened its pink mouth, revealing a flat, wide tongue before snapping its toothless jaws on the hopper. How excited I felt, how lucky, watching that small-scale drama unfold!

After lunch (delicious quesadillas made by my gringo *esposo*), I settled down to read a six-hundred-plus-page book by the dean of my future school—and wow, what a fantastic study spot I set up for myself. It was a beautiful day today: warm, little to no wind, almost no bugs, with drifting puffy clouds that left plenty of room for sunshine. Felipe helped me move his cot beside a rock circle shaded by pine trees. I lay there on a nice sleeping pad and a blanket, halfway in the shade, with just enough sunshine peeking through the pine needles to keep me warm. I could see the blue horizon of mountains to my west, the serene blue sky, and I could see and hear various birds all around me, including a hummingbird that took interest in the magenta color of my blanket. And speaking of hummingbirds—today the first rufous arrived! Felipe said they would arrive in July to wreak even more havoc on the bickering broadtails that drink from the feeders hanging on the cabin's porch. As promised, the rufous arrived on the second day of the month. It is an aggressive, golden-colored hummer with a distinct sound to its wingbeat. Its orange feathers are beautiful to behold in sunlight. Felipe and I sat watching another delightful drama unfold there on the porch. I can't wait to watch more of it in the coming days.

For our evening walk, we went southeast to a spot that overlooks a pond below a saddle on the main trail. It was spectacular, especially with the sunset light and the July clouds. There was a tiny rainbow just above the mountain, beyond the pond. We saw two deer grazing on the edge of the muddy gray pond below. Felipe told me he once watched a bear rolling around in the mud from up there. The sky turned all sorts of beautiful colors from blue up top (with a silver moon) to different hues of pink closer to the horizon. Breathtaking.

We walked back up the mountain at dusk and it was then, in the faint light, that we saw the owl. It lingered low on a ponderosa branch, staring at us, curious. As we three stood still for a moment studying each other, I felt an unexpected communion with this creature.

Now it's dark and we're sitting on the mountain by a campfire. The night is lit up by the half moon, small, bright, and high in the sky. A fair number of stars are visible. My heart is happy, my soul content. In a while I'll fall asleep in the embrace of my love, my companion in this wonderful life—with each moment on this mountain just a little more perfect.

flowers bloom in sky
like some hallucination
the fourth of july

Each year, around the day our republic celebrates having thrown off a tyrant and formed a democracy, the first rufous humming-bird of the season arrives at the feeders on the mountain. He announces himself with a great showy racket, his sound unmis-takable even before he comes into view. Until that moment, the broadtails have had the feeders to themselves, and an imperfect peace has prevailed, the birds taking turns on the perches, aware there is plenty for everyone, though the occasional bickering still breaks out. The rufous changes everything. His major tactic is a display of dominance, hovering menacingly with his tail flared and his brilliant red throat gorget flashing. The rest of him is a rusty orange of a sort seen nowhere else in nature.

Though the broadtails' social compact was never exactly utopian, it was based on a democracy of opportunity, and the rufous's arrival goads them into new forms of aggression seemingly at odds with their inherent character. His mere presence increases the chaos around the feeders exponentially. The broadtails don't have his flair, his swagger, or his shame-lessness, but they succumb to his talent for chaos just the same. The best mannered among the broadtails lack all conviction to fight the rufous, and the worst are full of a spastic intensity

july

that makes them look small and silly by comparison with him. Having set the broadtails against each other as much as against himself, the rufous wrangles a seat at the table while all around him the maelstrom plays out. If peace appears on the verge of reestablishing, the rufous renews his attacks. He seems to enjoy playing the bad boy. The attention it brings him only feeds his ego. If ever he finds himself alone at the feeder for more than a few seconds, he appears disappointed. He casts glances left and right, as if purposeless without a target to antagonize. To be ignored, one senses, would be for him the worst sort of punishment. So he makes certain he never is.

His dominance becomes pervasive and self-fulfilling. No move is made by the broadtails without full awareness of his presence. Though his method is brazen, the effect has a peculiar subtlety. Yes, he's loud, aggressive, garish, uncouth, and strangely colored, but to show up out of nowhere and transform an entire culture is no small trick. He's done it by taking up residence in the consciousness of all around him. Everyone has become reactive. They all wonder, fidgeting with anticipation and worry, what he might do next, where and how he'll attack. Their turns at the feeder become shorter and more anxious. The imperfect culture of restraint they'd achieved before his arrival now looks frayed beyond retrieving. Their awareness of a shared prosperity—easy calories at the sweetest mountaintop open bar in the world—is the only thing preventing outright civil war. But even that awareness feels as though it could be cast aside in a sudden spasm of violence. The line between uneasy peace and bloody chaos begins to feel as thin as a skim of ice that could crack at any minute. I am reminded, observing his antics, that suggestive parables exist all around me here, if only I pay attention.

I had ambitions when I first came to the mountain. I had plans and dreams, goals I thought of as professional. A few of them I even fulfilled: writing a book, for instance. And then another. And another. But the longer I sat and watched on the mountain, the fewer my ambitions became, until I ended up with only one so-called professional ambition: to sit on a mountain and watch. Okay, maybe two. To sit on a mountain and watch, and to sit on a mountain and listen. I never expected I would end up in dialogue with a mountain. But at the risk of sounding like I've gone woo-woo, here I am: in dialogue with a mountain. Every little thing helps make the whole, a beautiful Babylon of bees sipping water from the *huecos*, spotted towhees singing in the limbs of the aspens, Clark's nutcrackers jabbering and jeering in the branches of the pines. The vultures, the ravens, the hawks and kestrels, the wild turkeys, the ladybugs in their tens of thousands, the salamanders in their holes: all of them are a piece of the peace of the mountain, with which I want to be joined, now and forever. I remember Han Shan once more, writing his poems on the rocks and trees around Cold Mountain:

> Brown, my face, and white my hair,
> I love living on the mountain.
> Cloth robe wrapped around me,
> I accept what's coming to me . . .
> How could I try to imitate
> this world's vain schemers?

no one to impress
certainly not the squirrels
who judge me absurd

For reasons described below, I was asked to leave the mountain for a week unexpectedly. This being the story of a mountain as much as the story of one man's experience there, let us turn once more to Mónica in an excerpt from her journal, since she became the keeper of the mountain in my absence.

There aren't enough hours in a day. I'm alone on the mountaintop for the second day and it's all going by so quickly. I always want to do more than I can fit into the sunlight hours—even though I woke up just past six in the morning today.

On our second full day back on the mountain after his weekend off, Felipe got called by his boss to work Loco Mountain, which had become unstaffed since Jean left for a family vacation. Something about fire danger being higher over there than it is here. The order came as sad news to both of us since this would likely be my last full hitch with him on the mountain before I set off for grad school in New York. Felipe jokingly suggested there was nothing preventing me from simply staying on without him, to which my initial reaction was, "Ha ha, of course not." But by the time we took our evening stroll a few hours later, after we'd had an outdoor cookout that consisted of grilled carne asada with tortillas, *cebollitas, chiles torreados*, guacamole, and baked potatoes, followed by a dessert of s'mores, the thought of leaving such a magical place became more unbearable. So as we set out down a familiar path into the trees, I expressed my changing feelings. "Perhaps I should stay. My biggest concern is, who will feed me? You do all the cooking!"

As we advanced along our walk, so did my resolve. Our conversation grew more serious. By the time we returned to the mountaintop and settled by the fire pit for an evening campfire, we were working out the details.

As we prepared for bed, a thick fog enveloped the mountaintop in a matter of minutes. The haze looked spooky and unnerving as we watched through the bedroom window. I imagined being in the cabin alone and shuddered. I got into bed and nestled myself against Felipe's warm body, grateful for his presence. Sensing my uneasiness, he said, "There's nothing to be afraid of here. There's nothing out there that means you any harm." These were words he had spoken to me before, and while I believed him (somewhat), I couldn't quite find consolation in them. In the morning I'd have to make a decision, and once made, I had to stick to it, there was no turning back—too many preparations would be at stake. That night I had a dream of visiting a remote lookout that included a soak in a warm spring scented with wild herbs from the forest. It was very vivid and mostly pleasant—I'm not always that lucky with dreams. Almost instantly after I woke up, I knew what my

the mountain knows the mountain

decision would be: I would stay. I told Felipe when he woke up, and immediately we began the necessary preparations. He would not undertake his typical routine of stowing away his belongings and cleaning the cabin as he did before the arrival of his relief lookout. I would now be in charge of all that. Felipe briefed me on the details as he prepared a pot of green curry lentils that I could eat in the coming days.

By the time he had his stuff packed and on the porch, it was past two in the afternoon. We took a deep breath and said our goodbyes just a little ways down the trail. I walked back up the mountain with a box of kindling to start a fire in the stove the next morning. The mountain was all mine. It was the first time in my life all alone in the woods.

A few hours later the fog came back. I was sitting in the cabin reading when I saw its rapid encroachment. Without giving it much thought, I grabbed my camera and went outside. I remembered how fast it had moved in the night before and wanted to watch it firsthand in the daylight. The sight was mesmerizing. I felt more enchanted than spooked. I stayed out for probably an hour in the fog, climbing the tower and wandering the meadow, taking lots of pictures. Then I went back inside and prepared to read some more. I was probably indoors for only ten or fifteen minutes at most when I saw the fog begin to pull away. I grabbed my camera again and burst outside—I had to see this. It was clear the best vantage point would be from the tower. I climbed the steps faster than usual, watching as the mist withdrew at a steady pace. When

july

I reached the top I looked down at a blanket of clouds spread over the mountain range north of me with a few triangular treetops poking through. What I witnessed next is difficult if not impossible to describe in words. What I can say is that it was one of the most beautiful sights I have ever seen in my life. Every passing moment was more and more beautiful in its own unique way. First—simply looking down at a blanket of clouds gave me a thrill. Then watching those clouds recede and reveal the world beneath in a fantastical show of color and light simply took my breath away. The clouds seemed to caress the mountaintops, while the sun lit them in hues of gold, pink, purple, and orange. It was so overwhelmingly beautiful that I felt tears well up in my eyes. My chest heaved for a few beats. It was a powerful beauty that drew me in, took hold of me like a lover in a passionate embrace. I can't say I've ever felt anything quite like it—certainly not in response to the natural world. It was like one of those special moments Norman Maclean describes while fishing and being by the river, when suddenly everything sings.

My newest hobby is collecting "found poems"—that is, readymade haiku overheard on the two-way radio, the unwitting poetry of my colleagues in fire. A small sampling of favorites:

the mountain knows the mountain

report of a smoke
take a look out to your west
might be water dogs

seven souls on board
two and a half hours fuel
ten minutes en route

single snag on fire
cause appears to be lightning
no values at risk

on scene at this time
going into jumper ops
flight follow local

creeping in the duff
adjacent fuels the same
one- to three-foot flames

division zulu
requesting some bucket work
to cool the hot spots

we found an lz
configuring for buckets
confirm the dip site

july

    ops normal out here
continuing to bonepile
    all lines are holding

    tanker eight-nine-eight
inbound for load & return
    got one soul on board

    finished with mop-up
like to call the fire controlled
    back en route hq

There is something about seasonal work in a place with distinct seasons that deepens a person's awareness of mortality. The repetitions and rituals, the beginnings and endings. Lightning and fire, followed by serenity and renewal. Ephemeralities everywhere. Evanescence and reappearance.

    Each year I learn something new. This year? A pocket gopher and a salamander can peacefully coexist as subterranean next-door neighbors.

    the lichens drink fog
the mountain's shadow vibrates
    things a lookout knows

the mountain knows the mountain

My motto for living here: move slowly, and try not to break anything. My task in living here: reconcile the tranquility and violence of life on a mountain. My delight in living here: the mingled smells of rain and wildfire smoke upon the pivot of the season. The echoey call of the hermit thrush at dawn and at dusk.

> honor no border
> & salute no nation's flag
> the birds have it down

This afternoon I found a lizard broiled stiff in the plastic rain gauge nailed to the hitching post. Never having seen this flavor of catastrophe here, it took me a minute to puzzle out the scene. It had gone after a ladybug in the bottom, and could not make its way back up the slippery sides. An object lesson, as if another were needed, that the most unassuming piece of human infrastructure can have murderous effects on the nonhuman world.

> rain gauge waits & waits
> to justify its purpose
> i resemble that

july

I have not just a motto, but mantras, mostly borrowed.

Before enlightenment, chop wood and haul water. After enlightenment, chop wood and haul water.

When you reach the top of the mountain, keep climbing.

And my own koan: Only when you stop looking will you see.

think like a mountain
is a very tall order
first to think on one

The days pass in a haze of smoke like a gossamer garment cloaking the peaks and ridges, a soft and silky caress of the harsh skin of the land. Who foresaw the end of the Holocene being so dramatic and so beautiful?

canyons hazed over
by a miasma of smoke
a pastel sunrise

the mountain knows the mountain

Rain all afternoon. Only a few stump holes smoking on the now calm fires. The feeling of autumn in the air. Everything wet and green, the north-slope meadows a riot of bluebells in bloom. And even amid the abundance of beauty, an edge of melancholy creeping in—awareness that another season is about to end, after which it's back to the roar of the city, the devouring metroplex of El Paso/Juárez in all its burning hungers.

> there a thousand years
> turquoise bead chose this rainfall
> to reveal itself

This season has been particularly sweet with Mónica here for part of it. I enjoyed showing her so much of what I love about the place, the views that awe, the hidden grottos and stone altars, the creatures and their doings. She reacquainted me with reverence through her reaction to all she saw and experienced; she showed me things I'd forgotten, such as if you lie on your stomach very still, you can watch a short-horned lizard pick off ants with a lightning-quick tongue. We'll always now have the memory of sharing this sky island, our complementary views of it. A rare and beautiful secret between us, which can be summoned by two little words: the mountain. The mountain.

july

    cloud to cloud lightning
a jazz god playing cymbals
      way up in the sky

In the evenings this time of year a great stillness comes over the mountain. All one hears are the birds, and after they fall quiet, the occasional hum of a June beetle. The valleys and mesas are greening up with rain in the land below, and the distant ranges turn a deep cobalt under cloud shadow. I ought to be doing final revisions to my next book—but all I want to do is walk and look. It's a different mountain than the one I came to in April. Softer, more colorful with birds and flowers, more welcoming in its absence of wind.

     afternoon shadows
caress the rocking hammock
  with their cool blue arms

      the little dramas
fox trots across the meadow
   pack rat in its mouth

the mountain knows the mountain

    blue sky   cotton clouds
    breeze filtered through pine needles
    who would want to die

The mountain tree frogs have emerged at last. While lying in bed reading after dark, I heard the telltale croaking that announces: *time to get sexy, friends and neighbors* . . . The major hueco in the meadow is filling with water, rain falling since dusk, and the ancient impulse to propagate the species has been felt once more. Another marker along the season's arc. The days become extra precious for being numbered here—the hours like tiny jewels, alight with mystery.

    set a new snap trap
    grimly braced to take a life
    sly mouse took the cheese

Sitting in the outhouse just past dawn, door propped open with volcanic tuff, framed view of mountains forty miles off—serrated horizon pale in the haze—the CEO of something or other, the vice president of sunrise

july

> dazzle and presiding officer over lightning
> tightening the sphincter tries to have a thought
> deep enough to glorify a man on a throne:
> no court of men is supreme, for one,
> no house should have just one speaker,
> and the words <u>air</u> <u>force</u> can only mean
> anything decent when spoken in reference
> to the wings of a red-tailed hawk.

On my last days off, mainly for giggles but also because I like making lists and doing math, I tallied my lifetime earnings as a fire lookout. I discovered that in thirteen full seasons (my first having been a partial one), I made, on average, $10,862 per year.

Best year: $15,288. Leanest year: $7,419.

Yes, kiddos. If you are going to be a US Forest Service fire lookout, you had better learn to take the greater share of your payment in moonlight and dewdrops, and avoid confusing money with wealth. As the Buddhist layman Wang Fan-chih said long ago:

> Money's the thing that ruins humans.
> The wise will keep it at a distance.

the mountain knows the mountain

Most of us, granted time to reflect on the shape of our lives, can imagine a path or three not taken. I am no exception. I've imagined many more than that, probably because I've been given more time than most humans for idle reflection. Lest anyone believe I'm here thinking beautiful thoughts all the time, allow me to spin out one of my sillier counterfactuals. In this alternate reality, I've spent my days playing pied piper to disaffected denizens of the republic of terminal capitalism across multiple distributed platforms—a blogger of the first rank, a YouTube sensation, a star of the Twitterati, a Facebook friend to thousands, an email newsletter writer of astonishing prolixity, an Instagram influencer of the Mountain Time Zone Outdoor Lifestyle™—renowned for my musings on solitude and sky and the phenomenon of wildfire as witnessed from above in a modern anchorite's perch amid the harsh and lonely country of the Mexican-American borderlands . . . So it might have been had I acquiesced to the seductions of the age and set myself up with a smartphone and a signal booster, recorded my every move around the fire tower with a selfie stick, shared each nervous twitch and mind burp, gone live and shot them into the slipstream of the timeline for the benefit of a world still secretly desperate to believe in an honest (and not entirely inbred) way of life distant from cable television, watercooler wisdom, flush toilets, and internal-combustion motors. Why did I not seize the tools of the twenty-first century, join the streaming parade of compulsory performative narcissism, the awesome death-haunted spectacle of antisocial media, and make of myself a cannily curated brand: faintly bilious bard of the high peaks, mildly rebarbative recluse, charmingly dyspeptic apostle

july

of the ancient mysteries? What on Earth have I been doing here all these years, alone on a mountain on the government payroll? I believe the word for it used to be *living*. Nowadays, more like shirking. Possibly lurking.

Certainly I've been missing out, especially on the branded-merch hustle. Can't you just see it? FREAK ON A PEAK T-shirts, lookout-tower tchotchkes for your keychain, a line of sex toys inspired by lightning rods.

But as the novelist and poet Jim Harrison said, "Someone has to stay outside," a deceptively simple statement with more than one meaning.

I like to stay outside because I do not remain well—in mind or body—when confined by four walls and a roof, the exception being this glass box. I also prefer to stay outside the digital surveillance apparatus that's been built to monitor our every thought, our every purchase. Maybe I'd have capitulated by now if I thought being surveilled in this way would somehow make me a better person. On the contrary, it makes me want to act out. A cursory glance online confirms I am not alone in this.

More to the point, I fear I'm more susceptible than the average two-legged mammal to technologies designed with profound sophistication to prey on the brain's pleasure circuitry: mass-produced cigarettes, for example. I've added years to my life by living and working a two-hour hike and an hour's drive away from the nearest store that sells them. Someday science may show that I've done as much for my longevity by staying off social media. I only know that were I to make a run at the lifestyle of the very online, it would quickly be the ruin of my

the mountain knows the mountain

personality, such as it is—potentially quite entertaining for a moment, but in the end a debacle, a burning clown car careening into a Superfund site.

True, I have endured the deep soul sorrow of missing out on the greatest tweets and lunch photos of my generation, but my twittering companions here have done much to console me for my loss. In the past two days alone, I've either seen or heard these friends of a feather:

Dark-eyed junco	*Violet-green swallow*
Dusky flycatcher	*Black-headed grosbeak*
Clark's nutcracker	*Cordilleran flycatcher*
Western tanager	*Spotted towhee*
Common raven	*Mountain chickadee*
American robin	*Red-breasted nuthatch*
Zone-tailed hawk	*Brown creeper*
Turkey vulture	*Pygmy nuthatch*
Red-tailed hawk	*Townsend's solitaire*
Northern flicker	*White-breasted nuthatch*
Rufous hummingbird	*MacGillivray's warbler*
Steller's jay	*Hairy woodpecker*
Calliope hummingbird	*Hermit thrush*
Wild turkey	*Montezuma quail*
Broad-tailed hummingbird	*House wren*
Yellow-rumped warbler	*Band-tailed pigeon*

Lest I come off as holier than thou (too late, I realize!), I should acknowledge that I once flirted with crashing the Superfund

july

site. Several years ago, when a book I'd written was set to appear in paperback—the story of my first decade as a fire lookout and of this combustible landscape where I work—the book's editor suggested I join Twitter so I could tweet pithy things that would help move units. I didn't happen to share his belief that my being on Twitter would help sell books, nor did I care to join for amusement or pleasure, as using Twitter appeared even then neither amusing nor pleasurable. I had been to an open-mic night or two. Open-mic night times fifty million did not appeal.

Still, I wanted to satisfy the editor. I was a first-time author. I didn't want to get a reputation as the sort of writer who is not a team player, even though my book went on at obnoxious length about my disinclination toward being a team player.

I came up with what I thought of as an ingenious solution. I would not set up the Twitter account, although it would appear under my name. An editorial assistant at the publisher would manage the account on my behalf. Every so often, when I had something to say to the world, I would write on the back of a postcard and mail it to the editorial assistant on Fifth Avenue in Manhattan. The editorial assistant would take a photograph of the postcard, upload the image, and send it as a tweet via the account attached to my name. Not only could I tweet without ever logging on to Twitter, I could offload my unwanted labor onto a poorly paid and overeducated functionary, the secret dream of any proper art monster in our time. My identity as a techno-averse tree hugger would remain more or less intact, and I would send the assistant a bottle of excellent tequila every Christmas as a magnanimous gesture of thanks.

the mountain knows the mountain

When I proposed this in an email—my techno-aversion went only so far—the editor refused to dignify the idea with even so much as a one-word response. His silence said everything and came as a relief. Although I had thought my scheme rather clever, its rejection meant I was able to maintain my status as a conscientious objector. This identity is more dear to me by the day as I watch the best minds of my generation, writers whose work I once admired, destroyed by their machines, dragging their thumbs across the timeline at all hours of the day and night, hunting an angry fix. They might have written novels, memoirs, or essay collections. Instead they craft exquisite bumper stickers.

That's what happens when writing for readers—capable of sniffing out bullshit and attuned to layers of meaning—morphs into writing for followers: everyone suddenly develops the voice of a cult leader. The two-dimensional touch-screen portal makes everything it touches two-dimensional too, divided into right and wrong, good and evil, chosen and damned, beautiful and ugly. We have long known that information overload provokes an instinct for pattern recognition among its sufferers. The more we see, the less we truly *see*. Amid the sensory onslaught—the tsunami of data and shibboleth—the patterns become inscribed on our minds, until we can only see what we expect to see, everywhere we turn.

I'd have been smack in the midst of the bumper-sticker brigade had I persisted with a career in journalism, where an online presence is compulsory for career advancement. I've spared myself the temptation in part by swerving away from an early career in a tower in lower Manhattan to a much different career

the mountain knows the mountain

in a tower in southern New Mexico, and by being a seriously late adopter of the new technologies. I don't exaggerate when I say my flip phone has become my talisman as a thinking, feeling human being. It serves as a supremely inefficient tool for haranguing strangers or broadcasting bile, popular pastimes among us white guys—and the twin pillars of the social-media business model. I'm left to imagine how many clever memes I might have enjoyed over the years, how many sick burns I might have crafted for optimum virality, if only my gadget were internet capable. I console myself with the perhaps pitiable fact that I remain smarter than my phone.

But back to the more interesting question: what have I been up to all these years, aside from thinking inside this box? The major thing I've been doing, other than becoming a sky gazer, a bird nerd, and a hardcore bibliophile, is absorbing the when, how, and why of wildfire. It is an education that never ends in a dynamic landscape, and it demands a person *be here now* in a very literal way. Every day begins more or less the same. Wake and climb the tower. Look around. Make sure no sleeper smokes have puffed away in the night. Return to the cabin below and make coffee, a little oatmeal, or maybe some pancakes. Take weather measurements promptly at 9:00 a.m.: temperature, humidity, dew point, wind speed, cloud cover, visibility. Tally precipitation received over the prior twenty-four hours, if any. Report it all to dispatch. This takes me to 9:15 a.m., after which the hours are mine to fill as I please, as long as I'm mostly in the tower and never for a moment detached from my two-way radio.

july

Over the years I've developed a sixth sense for when I need to watch. Agency protocols advise that a full, 360-degree scan of the country be conducted every fifteen minutes. Like many rigid rules, it is soon discarded by someone with deep experience. There are occasions when a sweep every fifteen minutes is not enough. The wind is blowing too fiercely, or the lightning striking too frequently. What's really required is continual vigilance for hours on end without a break, right until the moment of sunset and maybe a little beyond.

Other times the country has been rained on, humidity is high, and the forest is lush and green, such that any fire that does start from lightning will only smolder quietly for a day or two inside the heartwood of the struck tree. In those conditions I might climb the tower once every two hours for a quick scan, then return to whatever maintenance project I was working on, whatever book I was reading, or whatever dream I was dreaming during an afternoon nap. There are even days when I wake up, sniff the air, and just know in my bones that there will be no fires. If personal experience is indicative, this sixth sense begins to be trustworthy around the thousandth day a lookout has spent on the job. That's also around the time you learn one of the deep secrets of this or any mountain—

> light moves through you if you wait
>   but you have to wait

the mountain knows the mountain

I've been sitting with that almost-poem for a month, waiting for the opening line to appear on the horizon of consciousness like a rising moon. No luck. But the right words come to you if you wait, though you do have to wait, often for a very long time.

Where was I? Most people assume that the work has been accomplished once the fire has been spotted, plotted, and called in to dispatch. Not so. It has only begun. Our firefighter colleagues rely on us for serious intelligence, what they call "eyes in the sky." Often, while they're still en route, driving or flying to the smoke, they'll want to know of any changes to our initial report. Is the fire growing quickly? Has the wind shifted?

Once on scene they'll continue to want updates on weather and fire behavior. If lightning is moving their way, they'll want a heads-up so they can take cover. If the wind shifts due to gusty outflows from a nearby storm, they'll want to know that too. And if radio frequencies clog with chatter from a dozen fires and they can't reach dispatch for supply requests, weather forecasts, or calls for additional resources on the ground or in the air, we are their communication link. They might never meet us in person—ten lookouts staff towers on this forest at any one time, scattered and reclusive on our peaks—but they know we've got their back. The job my colleagues do is as tough as jobs get and fraught with hazards of every sort. When their lives are literally on the line—the fire line, where they're face to face with the unpredictability of wild flame—they need me undistracted and fully present in the actual. They don't care about my politics, and I don't care about theirs. We're members of a team bound by common purpose, a thing rarer all the time in our culture of gig work and crude tribalism.

108

july

Once the rains come, though, I move in other realms:

> Floating in the blue,
> each ridge to the horizon
> bluer than the last—
>
> dayflowers unfold their blue
> in honor of dawn,
> too precious, that blue,
> to squander on night—
>
> the blue distances
> become a home to hide in
> when I'm blue:
> you might try it too—
>
> or has the icy shimmer
> of the screen light seduced you
> with its pseudo-blue?

Not long ago a friend of mine, a beautiful writer and about the most perceptive person I know, insisted (yet again) that I get with the program and ditch my flip phone. This initiated a conversation throughout which we talked past each other, the same way people do when using screens to communicate. I told him I was surprised that he felt so strongly about my duty to submit to the relentless zone of surveillance devised by our corporate overlords. He said he found it an embarrassment and a personal affront that I remained so dedicated to such an antiquated piece of hardware. I told him I wanted to focus my attention as a writer on creating works of art that had a chance at lasting, rather than on tossing off ephemera. He said he was living proof you could do both. I told him I had recently read a study that showed merely having a smartphone in the same room compromised one's cognitive capacity for anything other than the device's siren song of splendors calling out on the lower frequencies. He said my refusal to move on from a flip phone betrayed a "peculiar form of belligerence." I couldn't make him understand that my devotion to it represented quite the opposite, a hedge against my impulse toward belligerence.

Unable to sway me with his arguments, he resorted to emotional blackmail. He told me he was swapping out his iPhone for a newer model, and he feared that if he didn't give away his old one, a sometime lover of his would come by one day and filch it, pawn it, and use the proceeds to buy some crystal meth. He was still in the midst of a fragile recovery from his own addiction, and he didn't need the temptation. The implication was unavoidable. Either I took his phone, or I may as well hold the meth pipe to his lips.

Did I really have a choice? I suppose I could have pointed out that he had other choices. But he wore me down so ruthlessly, I capitulated. This is how I drew one step nearer to getting with the program—a program I fear inevitably ends with some kind of pogrom. My new phone sits off to the side of my typewriter, still lacking a SIM card. It makes a very fine camera. I tell myself I will only ever use it for that: snapping pictures (mostly of sunsets and cloudscapes) and taking videos (mostly slo-mo of lightning

july

strikes and time-lapse of wildfire smoke). But deep down I know I am already dancing with the devil. The day will come, I know it will, when higher-ups with the US Forest Service demand I either activate a smartphone with apps connected to real-time lightning maps and satellite heat-signature sensors, or make way for someone who will. The choice will be obvious. And the slope from there will be slippery all the way down.

I imagine I'll be ready for all the joys of the new media—sharing and connecting and trolling and doxxing, dialogue and ridicule and derision, scams and hacks and brand interactions, threats of murder and encouragement to murder myself—in another decade or so. My handle will be @pimpingmypeak because that's what I'll be doing, taking the place that's become my refuge and pimping it for all the world to see, encouraging the tourists to arrive en masse and pimp it some more via their own platforms. My DMs will be open, my musings antic and relentless, my self-curation crude but colorful. You'll know me at once from the faraway look in my avatar's eye—totally exotic, that look, having been trained for so long on things beyond my own palm.

> silhouette of peaks
> still there when i close my eyes
> still there when i dream

august

*I*n my earliest writings about the work here, I reveled in the license to laziness the job appeared to offer. That represented one of the key attractions of the lookout lifestyle, as alluring as the birds, the bears, and the stars. "The only way I've ever gotten along in this world is by staying away from it," the poet Kay Ryan once wrote. "I have had only enough character to keep myself out of situations that require character." Preach, sister!

To each rule, an exception. I soon realized that if the tower and cabin and all the associated infrastructure were not to fall into ruin, I would have to become the sort of man who did not embrace entropy as the natural state of things. I would need to make a handy human of myself, a process of reinvention that ran counter to my every native impulse. I would have to *work*—and so I did. I learned to repair a tin roof and a tongue-and-groove porch, perform simple carpentry, maintain rain gutters and a filter box for a water-catchment system, install a wood-stove chimney, patch crumbling concrete, replace window glass, chisel old glazing from window frames and reglaze them with fresh putty: all of these and more were part of the deal, part of the privilege of living here for an extended period of time each year. No one else was going to do it. And so I've achieved a certain baseline capacity for keeping the place intact, keeping my sinecure alive.

Everywhere I look, I see a project my hands have touched. I daresay the place appears the better for it, or at least no worse. It may also be the case that I am the better for it. More than once it has occurred to me to write a small monograph extolling the virtues of teaching oneself to fix things with one's own hands: a treatise on character and life amid the world of objects from someone averse to accumulating objects and largely devoid of character. I even have a working title: *Zen and the Art of Propane Refrigerator Maintenance*. But that's all. I haven't written a word of it. I know I never will. My indolence needs an outlet, a negative means of expression. A book I'm not writing: that's the ticket. A gift of nullity that keeps on giving nothing to no one.

> lazy vigilance
> alert while doing nothing
> harder than it looks

Haunting this hill for years, I am known
to the bears by my scent: that dude again,
still ripe. The vultures swoop low, sniffing
to test if I remain alive. Not the right ripe
for dinner. Flycatchers look at me with X-ray
eyes and see, in my skull, a dream home in waiting.

Seasons of fire, seasons of drought—retinas
alive to the movements of smoke; heart tempered
by the heat of flame—have made me
metaphorical. Annihilation. Rejuvenation.
Ash as prelude. Beauty from the burn.
I know how the caged bird gets singed.

Call me morbid, but I want to be like
a tree when I die, peeled to my essence
and host to some other life-form: moss,
lichen, woodpecker, tarantula hawk wasp.
Make of this corpus something nourishing.
Make it, at last, a place that feels like home.

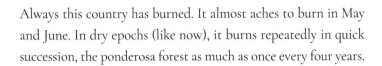

Always this country has burned. It almost aches to burn in May and June. In dry epochs (like now), it burns repeatedly in quick succession, the ponderosa forest as much as once every four years.

Fire is the norm, the equalizer, the guiding hand on the look of the land. It rearranges forest types. It cycles nutrients into streams and soils. It tickles the faces of the hills and makes magic happen in monsoon blooms of new wildflowers.

Fire in the southwestern United States has always set the stage for color in the fall foliage. The bronze of Gambel oak is nice, but no fall color beats the golden, high-country aspen, and nothing encourages the aspen like a big stand-replacement fire. Depending on a fire's intensity, aspen clones may sprout as soon as a few days or weeks later. In their first years they thrive in open sunlight, mingled with forbs and flowers in the rainy season, until decades on they form a filtering canopy that encourages an understory sprinkled with mixed-conifer saplings. When a colony of aspen becomes decadent after eighty or a hundred years, the conifers may encroach and flourish, unless the aspen burns first and replicates itself by sprouting new clones from the roots.

That's how it's always been, or so we told ourselves. A certain forest type at a certain elevation burns with such and such intensity; therefore x will grow back, or x and y, to be followed eventually by z—something definable setting the table for something else to come after it in predictable fashion. I think we simplified matters. I think we understated the complexity of true wilderness, which is, after all, "self-willed land." We spoke of climax vegetation when there was never any such thing, but rather an ecosystem always in flux. Be that as it may, if I'm allowed one prediction as a nonscientist, I'd say this: the past is

august

no longer a reliable guide to the future. Fire succession as we have come to understand it no longer applies with any certainty. The post-Pleistocene interregnum is ending. The planet is cooking. The fires are getting bigger and hotter. Forests all over the world are in the midst of die-off from drought, heat stress, beetle infestation, fungal attack, agricultural clearing, and wildfire. The forests of the American West—dependent on winter snowpack and a certain sensitive temperature range—are among the canaries in the coal mine. I often tell people that if you have an established fondness for them, go revisit them now. As in right now: this very day, this very hour if possible. If you haven't seen them but always wanted to, make your plans posthaste. The forests as we've known them won't be here long. They're vanishing with astonishing rapidity. The planet we've made by burning fossil fuels is inhospitable to their continued existence. If we were to make a model of the new globe and its atmosphere in the form of a snow globe, the snow would have to be rendered as ash.

My purpose in life appears to be watching trees die and seeing what comes next. Every walk in the woods now is an elegy in motion.

> little aspen shoot
> browsed by the mouth of the elk
> will you survive it

The berries are in their prime ripening. The bear scat is dyed with their color. I walk once more on the trail to the spring, which I rebuilt to repair damage done by the fire, and I find a juicy pile of shit in the middle of it. I take it as an ursine thumbs-up, a cross-species gesture of thanks for clearing the path to water.

> bear poop in the trail
> bright purple with gooseberries
> i crouch for a sniff

All these years here, beneath the lyrical evocations of life in a wild place, I have never entirely shaken the feeling of being perched on a knife-edge between beauty and violence. To the west, the Gila Wilderness: a land meant to remain unviolated by industrial tools for all time, a place where we vowed to practice humility and restraint and let the land be what it wants to be. To the east, the White Sands Missile Range: home to the Trinity Site, a place where humanity first tested the promise of instant mass death—the incineration of cities, the searing of human flesh. A simple swivel of my head and I behold a landscape of hope and a landscape of dread.

> called in a new smoke
> learned it was the missile range
> rehearsing end times

august

Memory is an indispensable companion in the midst of solitude. It takes you to surprising places, reintroduces you to people you'd forgotten. In the tower after lunch, for instance, reclining with my eyes closed, I am for mysterious reasons transported to that underground nest of urban cool the Village Vanguard and a night nearly twenty years ago when I sat in awe of Chucho Valdés at the piano with his large and beautiful hands, almost as beautiful as his smile, as he held the room spellbound with his joy in making music. I remember how I sat angled from his right shoulder so that I rarely saw his entire face—only between songs, when he turned to address the audience—though I had a perfect view of his hands at the keys and how they seemed to me then, and remain to this day, the most charismatic pair of hands I ever witnessed at work. I felt as though I were a key struck by them, and I vibrated so long afterward it was three in the morning before I could sleep.

My memory of his face also reminds me that I've never been able to trust, not entirely anyway, a human with perfect teeth. There was perfection in the slight imperfection of his.

> doing the laundry
> so much dirt in the bottom
> of the old bucket

the mountain knows the mountain

I find myself writing a subset of poem I call *I–ku*. Even by my elastic standards, they are marred by too much of the self and its ego, my fatal weakness as a wannabe haiku poet. By removing the line breaks, I can excuse them as prosaic forays into autobiography in seventeen syllables, though the 5-7-5 delineation remains:

If I weren't here, I'd be sitting in a bar, babbling like a fool.

I take the long view, but of course there's not much choice; it's what's on offer.

Asked my vocation, I say pyromaniac—but the harmless sort.

Naked in the dawn, secure in my solitude, I wander about.

I face off with wind, or perhaps ride the lightning—the sky's guinea pig.

I think all summer of things I'll eat in winter, none of which are beans.

The mountain trembles, or do I tremble on it—who knows which is which.

august

To mourn and to praise—my duties keep expanding the longer I stay.

I mourn the old growth, aware what's new this moment will one day be old.

Someday I'll be gone, but the mountain will remain—and so too the bears.

The unexpected thing about living on a mountain is that the beauty can hurt. It can be almost too exquisite. A mountain with a lookout on its apex seduces first with the view, but experienced over months and years, it dazzles with its life: the chirp and twitter, the hoot and whistle of the place, the animals and their inscrutable habits, the weather and its animate moods, the wild dramas of the heavens. Sideways rain, spiraling snow, pulsing wind, shooting stars, distant lightning after midnight, the roar of hail on the roof; the gift of ripe berries near the spring in late season, and surprise visits from friends bringing tequila and chocolate and cigars to share on the porch . . . Half the year, the half I'm not here, I keep a notebook whose tone makes Samuel Beckett sound like a life coach. I wiggle the scribble fingers, drag the hand across the page, and what's left behind is a strangled

the mountain knows the mountain

cry of despair for the mess my species has made of itself and the effect of our heedlessness on all the creatures big and small with whom we share this orb. How salutary to be reminded that this too is a piece of the world: the one we inherited and have not yet destroyed.

> clouds crown the mountains
> mountains rule the watersheds
> all else is wrinkles

I should—I take that back, not *should* but *could*, though probably won't—write a book of poems called *I Sit*. Each poem would begin with those words and slyly reference Han Shan and the practice of Zen meditation from the point of view of a modern fire lookout mostly unacquainted with the tradition of Zen meditation except by happy accident:

> I sit here looking
> out the window
> all day
>
> "a hell of a job of work"
> as my friend Tio Blanco
> likes to say

but it's what I do best
just sit here
looking

wanting nothing
harming nothing
so near *being* nothing

birdsong in the morning
and a pink moon
at dusk

Up at 5:00 a.m. beneath a moonless sky so delirious with stars it's as much silver as black. I wander the mountain in the predawn chill and wonder how many more years this body can get me here, miles from the nearest road. So many miles with a pack on my back . . . miles and miles over the years, with the aching joints to prove it . . . but after imagining the unknown future and roaming in memory over the past of this half-broken body, I bring myself around to the present. I am the opposite of a tourist, it occurs to me. Instead of going forth into the world, a consumer of experience, I sit in one place and allow the world to move through me, a conduit for experience. "The moon and sun are eternal travelers," Bashō wrote in *Narrow Road to the Interior*.

"Even the years wander on . . . every day is a journey, and the journey itself is home."

My journey, this day, begins with light washing into the sky on the eastern horizon, the first finger of sun reaching for a grip on the rim of the world. Breezes rising out of the canyons and dancing with the needles of the firs. Stars disappearing in the bluish scroll of dawn overhead. Thin bands of cloud turning pink over the desert, the mountains to the west still lost in a soft indigo haze. The serenity of this moment just before sunrise, when the country is poised to emerge from its slumber, but every little creature burrows deeper for a few last seconds of rest. Yes, dawn on the mountain is a cornucopia for the optic nerve. And at 6:30 a.m., the first voice joins me in praise of the moment: a Clark's nutcracker squawking in what sounds like sheer exuberance at the fact of being alive.

> scatter of feathers
> lying in the meadow grass
> hawk caught a flicker

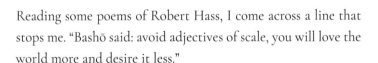

Reading some poems of Robert Hass, I come across a line that stops me. "Bashō said: avoid adjectives of scale, you will love the world more and desire it less."

A resolution for next year's journal: nothing enormous, nothing tiny. Just the things themselves.

the mountain knows the mountain

dayflowers wilting
a sudden bite in the air
flavor of autumn

waking in the fog
useless for the task at hand
my boss notices

I've been thinking about my allergy to bureaucracies, a nice piece of irony since I work for one. I believe I've puzzled out the beginnings of an explanation. It is the tendency of a bureaucracy to develop protocols in the service of high-minded aims—safety, fairness, equal opportunity, et cetera—and then build and tend systems that attempt to encourage the achievement of those aims. But over time, satisfaction of the protocols comes to dominate the day-to-day functioning of the outfit, and the systems become bloated and bog down the work. Bureaucracies become so dedicated to the process that must be completed before work begins that the process *becomes* the work, and less and less real work gets done. "Caring for the land and serving people" is our motto in the Forest Service. I have seen many colleagues become cynical and demoralized when they found themselves mostly serving systems. We are an agency top-heavy with overhead management and understaffed among the seasonal workers who actually spend time in the forests. Spending time in the forests is less and less valued because you cannot serve the systems there. What this means in practice is that trails on the map fall into ruin on the ground. Remote cabins and ranger stations are shuttered and left to decay. More employees spend their days under fluorescent light, and members of the public—who are, after all, the land's joint owners—almost never encounter a ranger in the woods. Closer to home, I think of the new outhouse my boss and I agreed was needed on this mountain six years ago, which remains unbuilt, lost somewhere in a labyrinth of paperwork.

I have been around long enough to know it wasn't always this way. When I first started as a lookout I asked my boss for some concrete mix to make repairs to the cabin. Then I left on days off. I returned four days later to discover he had packed six sacks of concrete in himself on three mules during my absence. I miss the gung-ho spirit of those old-timers. Now it takes four years of begging just to get a new wind sock that I can carry in myself.

A peculiar counterpoint to the new climate of inertia involves fire, where we err in the other direction by being too avid. Despite a change in philosophy that began in the 1970s and tried to account for a beneficial role for wildfire, the Forest Service was loath to give up its military-surplus toys (helicopters, airplanes) and just as loath to give up its habits (putting out every fire as soon as possible with every tool at its disposal). The disease of militarism infected the effort from the very beginning, resulting in a hundred-year war on fire, but it never should have been a war in the first place. Now we face the problem of sunk cost. Having fought fires so fiercely for so long, we can't all of a sudden *not*

the mountain knows the mountain

fight them, not when we convinced so many people that it was safe to build flammable homes in the midst of flammable forests. By allowing unnaturally dense fuels to accrue unburned over decades, firefighting perversely increased the need for fighting fires. The fire apparatus became the junkie in the family, addicted to its own bad habits, sucking up all the money that once went to wildlife restoration, trail maintenance, and so much other forestry work. That's what you get when you hand a bureaucracy the blank check of "emergency" funding for some specific purpose. It has every incentive to perpetuate the conditions that created the emergency, extending it indefinitely. Now it has its wish, as the severity of the emergency only deepens.

The war on fire has come to resemble the war on drugs: an exercise in hubris and a total failure waged at obscene cost in contravention of common sense and obvious alternatives. Why always the metaphor of war for our most troublesome problems—fire, drugs, poverty? Making war is what we do best, our republic having been born in war, our patriotic songs having long valorized war. It's our reflexive grasp at control. We define ourselves by what we aim to subdue.

Winning is another matter. We surrendered to the forces that profit from poverty. Drugs long ago won the war. Fire will too, if history is any guide. In the annals of expensive failures, our war on fire pales in comparison to our habit of raining war on distant lands at a cost in the trillions. It would be little more than a cultural footnote if it hadn't made for such dramatic imagery and caused so much disarray in fire-prone landscapes, priming them for eventual explosion. Everyone now knows this war to be a piece of lunacy, but no one in a position of real power has the guts to call it off and try a different way, or go back to the old way, the Indigenous burning practices we foolishly abandoned and denigrated. One exception is here in the Gila National Forest, where letting the land burn has a forty-year history that could instruct efforts elsewhere but mostly does not, because the old habits are too ingrained, and the new reality is too hot, too dry, and too explosively flammable to not scare the bejesus out of even the most dedicated professional pyromaniac.

> yearly reminder
> living inside a burn scar
> no escaping death

I notice a trend in this notebook as the season nears its end: the amping up of the social critic, as if the knowledge that I will soon rejoin the world below has caused me to gird myself for battle. Why adopt the pose of the pugilist throwing punches at straw men? As usual, someone else explained it better than I'm able to, in this case Henry Miller in *The Air-Conditioned Nightmare*: "This world which is in the making fills me with dread. I have seen it germinate; I can read it like a blueprint. It is not a world I want to live in. It is a world suited for monomaniacs obsessed with the idea of progress—but a false progress, a progress which stinks. It is a world cluttered with useless objects which men and women, in order to be exploited and degraded, are taught to regard as useful. The dreamer whose dreams are non-utilitarian has no place in this world. Whatever does not lend itself to being bought and sold, whether in the realm of things, ideas, principles, dreams or hopes, is debarred. In this world the poet is anathema, the thinker a fool, the artist an escapist, the man of vision a criminal."

It was not a world he wanted to live in, and neither do I, but I am soon headed there.

Beware the dude who only bellyaches about the human project and never confesses his own foibles. So: I made a visit to the district office on my last days off, to get a new battery for my two-way radio, and as usual found being there a profound bummer. By habit I brought a cigar as an excuse for ducking out the back door if anyone tried to get their hooks into me. It provided precisely the alibi I needed. I smoked and paced and plotted my escape from the premises, and then I stubbed the cigar and threw it in a dumpster back of the office. Word later came that I hadn't stubbed it out well enough. The butt landed in a pile of cardboard and started a fire. An extinguisher was deployed to put it out. The firefighter who discovered the smoke thought someone with a beef against the government had played a prank. But a cursory consultation of security-camera footage revealed me, the trusty lookout, smoking and then discarding my cigar in the dumpster not long before the flames came to life. Thus did I achieve the distinction of becoming the first Forest Service fire lookout ever known to have started a dumpster fire on government property, an exemplary moment in a distinguished career.

august

The best line from a season of reading comes from that grizzled
visionary Chuck Bowden, who looked me up and down and judged
me a literary cream puff the only time we met, maybe because
he'd written twenty books by then and I'd written one. "Imagine
the problem is that we cannot imagine a future where we possess
less but are more." Yes. Imagine.

Recipe: Wild Raspberry Tart

When the rain sets in & the sadness blooms, another season
in the (note)books, console yourself with your insider's
knowledge of the little nooks where the berries ripen last.
Grab a metal bowl & drum along its edge to set it humming
so the bears know you're coming. Walk in a one-person parade
on the meandering path to the place where the berries
grow in such abundance the bears blush at their luck.
(Or maybe they're tarting themselves up for the evening.)
Pluck the fat dark fruit that slips willingly into the hand;
leave the rest for some creature other than a man.
If you give a tug & the berry still feels snug,
let it be a while longer—the flavor will only deepen,

the sweetness grow stronger. Fill your bowl while
popping every tenth berry in your mouth, reverse tithing
as recompense for your miseducation in youth.

Eat a bug or two clinging to the fruit, protein complement
to the carbs. Careful with the twigs and their tiny fierce
barbs, the plant's way of making you wish you had paid
it more respect. Meander back up the meandering path
to the mountaintop. Exclaim, along with me, this mantra:
all praise & glory to the sun & the rain & the soil
for making this bowl of fruit so erotic it's practically
tantric what it's doing with your eyeballs. Open the pantry,
add a handful of sugar to draw out the juice, a pinch or two
of cornstarch for texture; use your hands as a mixer.
Lick your fingers. You've waited all summer for this,
your favorite of the season's rituals, sweetest for coming last.

As for the crust, it's always best to wing it & guess.
Say, four handfuls of flour, five pinches of sugar,
a tiny dash (or three?) of salt. If it comes out wrong
it is nobody's fault but the size of your hands or
the strength of your heart or the whims of the weather
or all the other claims on your attention just now.
Add a stick of butter, cubed, cut in with your favorite
sturdy fork. You want the fat in pea-sized pieces
if you've ever grown a pea, maybe Reese's pieces
if you're thumb ain't so green. Sprinkle ice water
over it, selfsame step for dealing with the naughty thoughts
you've been thinking of someone you ought not to.

august

Knead gently with your pink-stained hands. The dough, that is.
Make a round disk & flatten to the thickness of the tail of an
otter. Remember how your love looks in those underthings
you bought her. Cool it now. The dough, that is. Fridge or
freezer. Neither's easier but one is quicker. Let the dough
sit in a room that's known love. Like us, it turns soft &
pliant after some rest. Roll it out until the edges drape over
the lip of your skillet. Yes, well-seasoned cast iron is the thing
for the perfect flaky crust with a nice outer edge of crisp:
a pool filled with berries swimming in their own juices.
You want a very hot oven for the baking & just enough
bake time for a reverie of taking your sweetie to the edge
of prayer were she here. Your pink hands on her pink places.
Look into each other's faces to the end. Lick your fingers
again. Feel the heat of her heart. Do not burn the tart.

In late August the miller moths become desiccated and sluggish. I
can grab them by the handful where they cluster inside the supply
locker on the cabin's porch, among the paint cans and tools and old
coffee cans full of nails and screws and other hardware. Knowing
this, the dark-eyed juncos gather like winos outside the liquor store
at opening hour—postures of studied nonchalance, sideways looks in
my direction—any time they see my hand on the locker door handle.
Stunned by the sound of the door swinging on its hinges and light
flooding into their hiding place, a few moths try to fly away. The

juncos give chase in erratic flight patterns across the meadow, their beaks audibly snapping on the hunt. I toss a handful of moths in the grass like bread left for geese, and the juncos descend, scissoring the moths' dusty wings away with their beaks in order to isolate and dine on the juicy bodies. So much for harming nothing.

On the flip side, and from the point of view of the juncos, you could simply say that I'm passionate about customer service. It's a little game we play that pleases both me and them, a gratifying instance of cross-species collaboration—my life would be so much more pleasant if every last moth here were eaten—and for the juncos it represents a crucial part of their pre-winter diet: high in protein, rich in fat. I want them to be fat and happy. I want them to think of me as their friend and benefactor. At dusk the moths emerge of their own accord, and nighthawks perform the hunt, picking them off by the dozen, circling and swooping around the cabin until their white-barred underwings fade from view in the deepening dark.

And Sal the salamander: he gets his share of moths and hoppers when he pokes his head from his hidey-hole with what appears to be a smile on his face, as though in delighted anticipation of the meal to come, the meal he has trained me, like a good human pet, to offer on demand.

> seasonal migrants
> turkey vultures   hummingbirds
> and my typewriter

august

Yet again I've achieved my private goal for employment with the US Forest Service: fewer minutes spent in the district office (135) than days on the payroll (152) during a calendar year.

This feels like the place for profundity and summation, but I have no inclination toward either. What to say on this second-to-last day? I don't have much in the way of stuff, and that's okay. I have the love of Mónica, which is worth more than all the stuff in the world, and I have this job that lets me live amid an abundance of creatures, none of them trying to convert me, reform me, or separate me from my meager pile of US dollars. I own an old pickup, an Olivetti typewriter, and two thousand books, most of no special value to anyone but me—the tangible record of my curiosity. I carry a notebook wherever I go, the current one my forty-ninth in two and a half decades of filling them. That makes the next one special, a landmark of sorts.

Best to have no goal, feel no pressure when scribbling for the edification of your own self. I don't see how I could have done it any other way. A lot of ink. A lot of paper. A lot of nattering on. But there exists among the accretion of tedious nonsense and solemn pronouncements the occasional burst of music and laughter, the odd insight; perhaps, too, a message in a bottle for the future, if anyone eventually cares to recall the names and habits of a few of the other life-forms that once enlivened this world, before humankind commandeered the ark of the Earth like a band of pirates, surveyed the passenger list, and tossed most of the occupants overboard, having judged them unworthy of sharing the voyage with us.

Take the truck away from me: that would hurt, but I could put my thumb in the air. Take the books: that would hurt more,

the mountain knows the mountain

but there would remain libraries. Take my notebooks and you take the blueprints for how I built a soul. Melancholy and misshapen, yes—but something resembling a soul nonetheless.

down comes the wind sock
that most melancholy chore
the season has passed

The Fire Finder is covered, the propane turned off, the cistern locked. The rodents are free to claim their time-share.

midnight calling card
in the corner of the room
one little mouse turd

afterword

a visit to the mountain, one year later

BOBBY BYRD

My wife Lee and I founded an independent publishing company, Cinco Puntos Press, named after the Five Points neighborhood where we live in El Paso, Texas. We began in 1985. Publishing has been a remarkable adventure, taking us to many new places of the imagination and spirit that we hadn't known before.

That's how we met Phil Connors, a writer in the great tradition of Ed Abbey, Gary Snyder, Charles Bowden, Doug Peacock, and so many other heroes of mine. Writers who have given their lives to Wilderness, recognizing it as essential to the human experience. Without it we are lost.

In October 2018, Cinco Puntos released Phil's third book, *A Song for the River*. A few months before its publication, the intimate process of working with an author led us up to his mountain overlooking the Gila Wilderness, where he has been a fire lookout since 2002.

the mountain knows the mountain

Phil had invited us to join him for two nights in his little cabin perched at ten thousand feet above sea level. He wanted us to see the watershed that had given birth to the book we had worked on together. We didn't have to carry much. Phil promised us a warm bed to sleep in, good food, mountain silence, and great conversation. He kept his promise tenfold.

It's a five-mile hike and an altitude gain of two thousand feet from the place where we left the car at the trailhead. Not much for younger folks, maybe, but Lee and I are in our seventies. We looked forward to the journey with excitement but some trepidation. We had both expanded our workout regimens in El Paso—Lee added the steep hill in McKelligon Canyon to her morning walks with her walking buddy, Martha, and I wandered up the rocky trails in the Franklin Mountains. We both wanted to be ready.

Our journey was to take us through the burnt trees and stubble left behind by the ferocious Silver Fire of five years earlier, a fire that required a helicopter to pluck Phil from his outpost ahead of the flames. We walked through the rebirth, all sorts of new plants and habitat sprouting from the ashes of the fire. For the first couple of hours the trail was pretty easy—a gradual incline, damp earth, wonderful views on either side of the ridge the trail followed. Lee was proud. She even said something like, "I think Phil was fooling us. This is easy!" A few minutes later she learned that the mountain gods have ears. Drum rolls of thunder started tracking us up the mountain, herding along dark and darker clouds like obedient cattle. Then the rains came. Drizzling at first, holding off long enough for us to put on our raincoats. After that

afterword

the storm began to pound us. The trail, of course, turned rocky, and the path transformed into a small creek, the two of us wading upstream. The rain kept coming, we kept walking.

Halfway up, we met two women—a mother and daughter—coming down. They hadn't made it to the top. The rain pushed them back. We quickly compared notes in the rain, then moved on. A minute or so later the trail crossed over a huge rock slide, but thanks to the 1930s Civilian Conservation Corps and wilderness ingenuity, a retaining wall made the crossing easy for the old folks. No concrete, just stones, one on top another, eight feet high, leaning in against the mountain for all these years. To build it, the workers had to first pull away stones to clear the path and make space for the wall, then, using the same stones, build the wall. It's wilderness, so it was all done without machines, just picks and shovels, hands and arms, muscle and bone. And here it was, eighty or so years later, still doing its job. I wanted to take a photo, but Lee wanted to push on.

She was right. It was raining and we were getting cold. We stuffed peanut butter sandwiches in our mouths and kept on walking, sloshing along the trail—one step after the other, one step after the other. The next breath and the next breath. It's the only way to walk a straight line up a crooked mountain. That's what the ancient mountain monks of China always said, drunk and laughing at fools like us.

After another forty-five minutes or so, while walking across a saddle, the Gila Wilderness to the west, the valley of the Rio Grande to the east, the clouds above, the mountain beneath them, rain coming down, I heard something behind me. Cocooned inside

the mountain knows the mountain

my raincoat, I couldn't figure out what the sound was. Something was close behind. I turned around. It was Lee, passing me. "You're walking too slow," she said. Up she went, and for the rest of the journey, there she was in front of me, maybe twenty yards or so, pulling me along by her very presence. I was proud. She was my guide up the mountain. Later she would say, "I was cold and tired. I knew Phil was up there warm and dry in a cabin with a fire going. That was all I needed to know."

Phil's mountain was like every mountain—the last part was the most difficult. The climb was steeper, switchbacks carrying us back and forth through the tall and very wet grasses of summer. Now the forest was huge around us, the trees untouched by the Silver Fire. Wild raspberry bushes grabbed at my hands. The rain washed the red blood down into the ground. I was counting my breaths, counting my steps. Breathing in, breathing out, heart pounding. I had to stop every hundred steps or so. Catch my breath. Then it was every fifty steps. Every ten breaths. I knew we were close to the top. But the top never seemed to come.

Had we gone too far? We kept going. Lee was up ahead, looking around. I looked around too. Something blue was coming down the mountain. It was Phil in his blue raincoat. Bearded, a big smile on his face. He had come looking for us. Yes, we had missed the first side trail up to the top. It was back there, veering

afterword

around a thick tree where we hadn't seen it. "Not to worry," Phil said. "There's another little spur trail just a bit farther." After a hundred yards or so, a big meadow opened up before us with a view of his little cabin. The fire tower stood near the cabin like a skeleton in the drizzling foggy daylight.

His is a little house, a casita, maybe fourteen by twenty-four feet, one open living space with a small bedroom tucked in the corner—Phil's home, truly, the way he knows every nook and cranny of it, like the captain of a small sailboat where space is precious. For the next two nights, he made it our home. That's how we felt. Phil had a fire going in the wood stove, a clothesline strung above it so we could begin drying our clothes and socks. Coffee was brewing, welcoming conversation, good stories, laughter.

When we got warm we climbed the steel stairs up the tower, passed through a trapdoor and into a small room of windows fifty feet above the ground. It was spectacular. Phil pulled down a map pinned to a piece of plywood, showed the tools of his trade for triangulating the position of a fire, and pointed out the mountains and landmarks in the great vistas around us, all of it huddled in clouds and fog.

Lee was the editor of *A Song for the River*. Because she had read it so many times and knew it so well, she asked about mountains and people, the sad but enduring stories that are the subject of the book. The conversation wandered here and there but never far from where we sat on Phil's mountain, above the Gila Wilderness and the wild river that runs through it. These are the body, blood, and bones of Phil's work, the compass of his understanding of himself and the world. The earth and the sky above it. Human beings are simply brief sparks of light. This is a place for teaching ourselves the breadth of scale and time.

Daylight slipping away, we came back down and Phil cooked us a wonderful hot dinner, talking while he chopped and diced, measured and simmered, all the while swapping stories, laughing—high-country performance art at its best. The dinner was delicious. And the encore was homemade peanut butter cookies and a shot of whisky poured over an ice cube from his propane fridge. We were roughing it, baby. I giggle now, writing this, even to think about it.

We were exhausted. Aching bones. Sore muscles. It was early for us, but we were ready for bed. Phil was kind enough to give up his cozy bed for the two old people. He put a five-gallon "piss bucket" beside us in the little room so Lee wouldn't have to make nighttime treks through the very dark cold to the outhouse a good hundred feet or more away. I am no fool. I likewise took advantage of the excellent facilities. Three times, in fact.

Phil, for his own lodging, decided to set up a tent within a circle of stones and beneath a canopy of giant pines. A friend of his had built the stone circle a few years before, but now the space looked ancient and sacred, with lichen on the rocks. I envied Phil the freedom of mind and heart to move outside under the stars, but at the same time, after that rain-soaked hike, I was so happy to be warm under the covers of his little bed, sleeping next to the animal warmth of my wife. Yes, yes, we were home atop Phil's mountain, his casita a little boat tethered to the lookout tower and bobbing in the waves of the cosmos.

I slept well, even with Lee and me doing our little domestic dance, one climbing over the other to pee in the bucket, the other sleepyhead moving against the wall so the one who had just peed could slide back into bed with ease. I should have gone outside to look at the stars, but my job was to sleep, and to pee when the time came. That's all, and that's enough on the first night. Waking in the early morning, it took me a bit to remember where I was. The bed was different, the morning light was different, the air we breathed was different. Clean. Pure. Very early I heard the hummingbirds outside the window sucking up the sugar water.

Oh, yeah, oh yeah!

Before Lee got up and Phil started fiddling with the daily habits of life in the kitchen, and before the rain started climbing up the mountains from the south, I went wandering in the wet meadow. I carried along a pillow, I found a good rock, just the right height, and I sat in meditation for twenty minutes. Perfect. High-country meditation is easy. You just sit there. It's a lot like lowland meditation. You just sit there. It's different in some ways but mostly the same. Sitting there. I did hear the hermit thrush—a timid bird, Phil tells me, true to its name, at least physically if not musically. The little guy does love to talk, explaining the secrets of the universe, especially in the morning when the old white man is listening!

the mountain knows the mountain

I went back and found Phil starting coffee and making pancakes. My gosh, pancakes with butter, maple syrup, wild raspberries! He had picked the berries yesterday, he said, when he was waiting for us to get our asses up the mountain.

Saturday was an old-school Sabbath kind of day. A day of rest. An off-and-on drizzly day with blue sky every once in a while, a little bit of wind. Lee was still asleep, so Phil and I read poems to each other. I read a poem from Africa from a *librito* I had packed with me. Phil read me one of Wendell Berry's Sabbath poems. Thanks to Phil, Wendell Berry shadowed us the whole day, his poems, his ideas, his beliefs in the old ways.

> To rest, go to the woods
> Where what is made is made
> Without your thought or work.
> Sit down, begin the wait
> For small trees to grow big,
> Feeding on earth and light.

Turned out that Phil had been thinking a lot about Wendell Berry. That's one of the perks of the job. Thinking, reading, thinking about the reading. He can multitask by looking up from a book now and then to survey the mountains for smoke. And he can spend a whole summer immersed in the work of a single writer because he's got the time. One summer it's Cormac

afterword

McCarthy. Another it's James Baldwin. Then Annie Ernaux, or Toni Morrison, or Gabriel Garcia Márquez. Or pairings of different writers whose virtues are heightened by contrast: Ellen Meloy and W. G. Sebald. What a privilege, that sort of deep reading.

Wendell Berry is a singular poet, essayist, novelist, and farmer. In today's terminology, he might be called a Luddite and a backwards old coot. He doesn't use a computer. Good for him. He's a practicing, anti-institutional Christian, and all his work flowers from a deep spiritual understanding that we are here to care for the Earth in all its wildness and beauty. This is how he worships. I can dig it. And honor it.

In the bottom of my backpack, I carried several ounces of my friend Robert Washington's ashes in a Ziploc bag. Bob died April 10, 2016, in El Paso, although he lived most of his adult life in San Antonio. He said he wanted to come home to El Paso to die. That's why he was there. I had become an off-and-on helper and caretaker. He had adopted Lee and me years before because we often traveled to San Antonio to exhibit at the Inter-American Book Festival. We'd even stayed at his magical house full of Mexican and folk artifacts. Turkeys, feral cats, opossums, and raccoons wandered around outside in an enchanted and very small wilderness.

In his later years he had become a practicing Tibetan Buddhist, traveled to Thailand to meet the Dalai Lama and, indeed, took his vows, wearing his mustard-colored robes and strings of beads (malas) hanging from his neck and wrists when he went out into the world. He had become huge, well over three hundred pounds, and so his ashes were plentiful and way too much for the urn that he chose for the purpose. That urn now sits off to the side of the altar at the Both Sides / No Sides Zen Center in El Paso, a place Bob felt a fondness for. But there were ashes to spare, even though I gave them out freely to friends who asked. Bob, I knew, would be honored to have his ashes scattered high in the Gila Wilderness on Phil's mountain, which is what I intended to do.

I announced my purpose as we finished our delicious pancakes and wild raspberries. Phil was glad to know of Bob, glad too that this place would become a home for some part of him. He said he knew the perfect place. After he finished cleaning up the dishes, we followed him through the wet morning grasses to the southeast. There's a hueco less than a hundred yards from the cabin, a depression in the earth that gathers water after rain. Sometimes, if there's a big rain for a good period of time, the hueco becomes a small pond and little frogs burst into the world. The rain Lee and I had walked through was not enough to fill the whole hueco, but it was enough to fill a small stone basin in its center, maybe two feet wide and a half foot deep. The water was cool and clear, true mountain water.

This, Phil said, is where he scattered the ashes of his friend John. A fellow lookout way across the other side of the Gila Wilderness, John had been like a brother to Phil for a decade and

afterword

more. One day, a year after the Silver Fire, John and his old horse had tumbled off the mountain to their deaths. Nobody knows how it happened. Maybe the horse had a heart attack. Who can say? Phil tells this story in *A Song for the River*. But right then all he wanted me to know was that this place was a holy spot, and he was honoring my friend Bob and his friend John by leading us here to scatter Bob's ashes so they could join with John's.

I took out a small handful of the white-grey ashes, full of tiny bone shards, and dropped them into the clear cold water. As the ashes sank to the bottom, I stirred the water with my hand and it became milky, sediment slowly dissolving back into the earth. I had meant to bring several prayers to read, but I had forgotten them in the hubbub of leaving. I mumbled a few words to myself in almost silence as the ashes dissolved. The three of us were confused by what to say or what not to say. Each of us has our own understanding of death and the ritual of death, so each of us said something quietly, hesitantly. That was okay. It didn't change the moment, the ashes clouding the water.

Here's Bob's evening prayer from the Tibetan Buddhist tradition, I'm sure modified for his own voice:

> I pray to you from the bottom of my heart.
> Please regard me with compassion from afar
> In this life and the next, as well as in the intermediate state.
> I make you my haven of hope.
> Just now while I am alive in the human realm
> Is an opportune moment to grant your blessing.

the mountain knows the mountain

Bob practiced old-school Tibetan Buddhism, all the bells and whistles, the long chanting, and he enjoyed contemplating rebirth. Not me. That has always seemed sort of silly. Like Gotama said, if you haven't done it, don't talk about it. But these were not my ashes, not my bones. So I happily repeated his death prayer. I don't know to what or to whom he was praying. I should have asked him while he was alive, but I'm down with Walt Whitman in thinking it muddies the water of compassion and friendship to argue about God or spiritual practice. But since I was the last guy standing in our friendship, I read his prayer at the memorial gathering for him and followed it with one given to me by a Zen buddy:

> Because of the ceaseless action of cause and effect,
> reality appears in all its many forms.
> To know this fully liberates all who suffer.
> All beings appear just as we do from the one,
> and pass away as we all do,
> after a few flickering moments or years of life
> back to our original unborn nature.
> Truly our lives are waves
> on the vast ocean of true nature
> which is not born and does not pass away.

afterword

It was still chilly, a little bit of drizzle, so Lee went back to the casita to read and nap. A ten-thousand-foot mountaintop is as perfect a place as you will find for napping. Phil was still on the clock, so he had chores to do. I went off with the rest of Bob's ashes. I thought I would scatter them from the watch tower, but halfway up I pinched some from the bag and let them go. There was no wind, so they fell straight to the ground, some of the bone shards bouncing off the steel girders. I could hear Bob saying, "Well, this is no fun," so I climbed back down and went looking for more appropriate places.

That wasn't hard. Phil had showed me a spot beneath a tree and against some rocks where he had found a couple of potsherds. You could still see them there. Perfect. I scattered another handful of ashes for *los ancianos* of the mountaintop. Then I walked down the trail and found bunches of low-lying flowers, yellows and pinks, some Indian paintbrush too. Bob loved flowers, so the remaining ashes and bone shards went among them, little mountain flowers enjoying a drizzly day at ten thousand feet above the seas girdling the ancient crust of the earth. I kept mumbling prayers to myself and talking to Bob. It was a fun journey. Turned out I had things to say.

I went back to the casita and took a nap.

the mountain knows the mountain

That was the kind of day it was. I was at peace. Just wandering around on the top of the mountain. Drinking coffee at the table in the cabin. Talking with Lee and Phil. Poems and ideas. Wendell Berry. Gary Snyder. Memories of growing up. Fathers. Mothers. Brothers. Sisters. The lives and deaths of Phil's friend John and others he had known and admired who loved this wilderness as he did. The mountains and the fires in the mountains. All the ghosts that follow each of us around in memories. Drizzle coming and going. Damp rocky earth. Grasses wet with mist. A halo of pine trees surrounding the open meadow, surrounding us. Ponderosas. White pines. Black rock with a growth of green lichen.

"Look here," Phil said on one of our little walkabouts. From under a rock, he pulled a weathered ornamental tin box. Inside was a Ziploc bag and inside the bag was a very short note. A woman's writing announcing the ceremony of a man and a woman, a couple, who had brought the ashes of their dog Toto to the top of the mountain. This was one of their favorite hikes—a woman, a man, and their dog. Nothing else in the note. Just the tin box, the Ziploc bag, and the note hidden very privately under a rock. The hiding place was at the foot of an outcropping of stone, bench-like, a wonderful place to sit, looking out to the west over the Gila Wilderness with all its complexity of mountains and creeks, and the Gila River which drained it all. They must have scattered the ashes in the wind, then talked about their dog, held hands, maybe said a prayer.

Years later Phil sat on that same bench of black stone, reached down, and found this remarkable artifact. Now he showed it to us. We placed it back into its mountain cache.

afterword

Good people, good dog, good mountain.

Wilderness mountains secrete all sorts of human memories. Yes, we should not try to fix wilderness, but listen to it. Deeply. And return to it once we are ash.

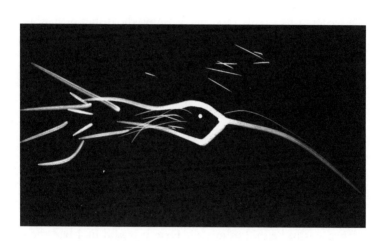

For entertainment, there were always the hummingbirds. Phil had two hummingbird feeders hanging off the beam on the porch. It was crowded with broadtails all day long. Each feeder had ten perches, and the hummingbirds would swoop in, taking their turn, sometimes filling every perch on both feeders. Ten little birds feeding at the sugar water next to ten little birds feeding at the sugar water. Like a nursery rhyme. A brief moment of silence, then they would scatter, sometimes one by one, sometimes in a

the mountain knows the mountain

great humming cloud. It was wonderful, hypnotic entertainment. The broadtails, the early summer population, were not bothered yet by the small but mean-ass rufous hummers who come scaring the bigger birds off their feed. Phil said he'd seen other varieties, some rare—black chins, calliopes—but we were satisfied with the pedestrian broadtails, which we have on our own front porch in El Paso, although certainly not in such numbers. I made a drawing of one on my phone with my Zen Brush app. For Phil, refilling the feeders was a daily task, like washing the dishes or hauling water. Zen in its way too.

There were other tasks, and we performed them. We sat in the meadow and looked at rocks. We wandered some, but not too far. The huge sky kept changing, clouds coming and disappearing. We watched that too. Lee and I were happy just being there, bone tired but content. Mountains are made for haiku, I realized, not long journal pieces like this. Or maybe they're made for both, to be mixed together, a journey through time and space like the haibun of the old Japanese masters. Maybe they're for saying what needs to be said in just the form it is said in. I had these thoughts, and I didn't even know that in his worn black notebook sitting there on the kitchen table in the cabin, Phil was revising his own version of a haibun based on his previous summer on this very mountain.

The mountain teaches if you pay attention. That's what Phil's books are always saying. Being up here alone, watching for fire, keeping himself warm, feeding himself, walking around, sleeping, Phil could not help but become immersed in the mountain's rhythms, ego washing away downhill like bits and pieces of dirt

afterword

and stone. Trees, flowers, grasses, animals, bugs, birds, human beings—all the fauna and flora of a mountaintop are born, live their lives, die, and are replenished. When I was scattering my friend's ashes among some little yellow flowers sprouting in a stone crevice, I remembered the Zen koan of "Yun Men's Golden Wind."

> A monk asked Yun Men,
> "How is it when the tree withers and the leaves fall?"
> Yun Men said, "Body exposed in the golden wind."

I study koans with my friend and Zen teacher Chodo Campbell. When we arrived at this koan, Chodo told me it was one of his favorites. I was surprised. It's not one of the famous ones like "Joshu's Dog" or the one hand clapping. It seems so obvious—things change. Well, duh! But in koan study, intellectual answers are no good. A teacher wants a flash of understanding, a physical or emotional expression that speaks to the heart and mind simultaneously. An instant of realization, of awakening, a place without borders.

It took me a while to pass through Yun Men's gate. In fact, I'm still working on it and probably will be until I too slip into that golden wind.

The Japanese have a word, shin, for this place of understanding that resides deep in the human psyche. It means something like "heart-mind," although this is not a completely accurate synonym of shin. There's really no English word that works. "Soul" should work, but we are taught (or at least I was) to think of soul as unchanging, as something, like God, that doesn't die. Instead it goes to heaven or some other place in the cosmos. But in the Buddhist worldview, everything changes moment to moment, and everything of course dies. The mountain dies. The Earth dies. God dies. My friend dies. When I listen to the Charles Mingus tune "Better Git It in Your Soul," I feel that his jazz is talking about shin.

> mountain stone is home
> for lichen, tiny flowers
> and a friend's ashes

The minimalist poetics of the haiku form has roots in this notion of shin, the instantaneous expression of reality, a snapshot of the poet's heart-mind as she sees the world as it really is, without the interference of ego. An impossible task, but oh well, that's what koans and haiku are all about. Thus, I was not surprised when Phil, who has never considered himself a poet, shared his haiku with Lee and me, first a handful of them in the manuscript of *A Song for the River*, and later in correspondence and conversation. The mountain was allowing him to write haiku, and the mountain was teaching him, and all of us, about "Yun Men's Golden Wind."

afterword

That night Phil made spaghetti and meatballs. I had packed in an orange at his request, and Phil used it to concoct an old fashioned with bitters and bourbon on ice. We made jokes and laughed, feeling looser with the booze. That night, when we were going to bed, Lee admitted she had been worried ahead of our visit. With the continual uncertainty of rain, we would only have conversation to spread our time across the day. She worried it might be boring for Phil and for us.

Not so. Conversation came and went, like the clouds and the sun, the rain and the blue sky. That night I learned a great secret. I didn't need to sit on the bucket to pee. I just picked it up and held it. I giggled as I climbed back into bed, crawling over Lee. It would be her turn next, but she'd have to squat.

The next morning was going-down-the-mountain day. I woke up as light began filtering over the Caballo Mountains, way across the wide Rio Grande Valley. Over there too are the San Andres Mountains, and beyond them the Sacramentos. A huge magnificent vista dotted with clouds.

Phil made us oatmeal, and we continued our human chattering. Saying goodbyes. *Abrazos.* We packed up and left, taking a few more photos along the way, remembering the skies, remembering the casita. Down we went, step by step, breath by breath, an animal rhythm to be sure, in our own heads and hearts, but together in the big world—Big Mind, as Suzuki says. We stopped here and there for a water break, talking a little bit, chewing over our visit like cows with their cud, such a pleasure.

But over us we could see the dark clouds coming again. Been there, done that.

And we didn't want to do that again. We pushed ahead and, lucky us, the rains and thunder came tumbling down just as we got to the car, reminding us that we were human beings on a mountainside swirling around on the planet Earth.

postscript

the last letter

Below is the last letter I wrote to Bobby Byrd before his death in July of 2022. Wrapped up in the drama it describes, and mostly out of reach of the postal service for weeks on end, I did not have the chance to send it before a fast-moving stomach cancer claimed him at age eighty. The fact that it sits in my files unsent serves to illustrate the letter's ultimate insight: the impermanence of all things.

June 14, 2022

Dear Bobby,

I hope you don't mind my dropping a big smoke bomb on you. I've been relocated from my fire tower—not evacuated by helicopter this time, but definitely ordered to leave—and reassigned to a different tower, twenty-five miles north, where our ongoing mega-fire has already swept past and gone cold.

the mountain knows the mountain

It's a waiting game to see when it reaches the mountain you and Lee visited four years ago. Here at 8,800 feet above sea level, the smell of burned pine permeates my every waking moment and perfumes my dreams, acrid and bittersweet, not unlike the dreams themselves. It's a mosaic burn up here, with pockets of black where trees torched out in crown fire, pockets of orange-red needles where the trees didn't torch but were nonetheless killed or stressed, pockets of green where the fire stayed on the ground in the grass, and even some places the fire left totally untouched. That's how it typically goes in the ponderosa country. Ponderosas evolved to burn and survive. Up above the ponderosa belt, to the south of here, on the crest of the range, it's obvious what happened to the high-country mixed conifer. It's gonzo. Totally black. That, too, is how it always happened, the mixed conifer tending to burn in stand-replacement events. So say the tree-ring scientists, and I happen to trust them. They also say that as far back as they can look, these events tended to happen in discrete pockets of a few hundred or a few thousand acres at a time. The high country was generally moist from snowmelt well into summer, and fires never really went berserk there, at least until the twenty-first century and the onset of our current mega-drought. The tree-ring scientists tell us it's the most severe drought in more than a thousand years, amplified by global warming. Now the mixed conifer is going away in thirty-thousand-acre chunks at a time, and it ain't coming back. That has always been my favorite of the forest types in this country. If I'd fallen first for the ponderosa, maybe I'd feel less discouraged.

postscript

One month and one day into our epic mega-fire, I feel like I've been through fourteen rounds with a bruising heavyweight. Now it's the beginning of the fifteenth round, the end in sight but not here yet, the body blows coming fast and furious, and it's all I can do to stay on my feet and not curl up in the fetal position. Today the Black Fire burned into one of my favorite places on this ailing Earth, which tipped me down the slippery slope of nostalgia. The first time I tried to get to the magic canyon, sixteen years ago in the month of August, I failed. My friend Larry McDaniel and I had been told there were trout in the stream there, but by the time we went looking for them, drought and heat had sent them way upstream into the cold headwaters. We got lost on that trip, bushwhacked through some god-awful country, lost an entire day and a pint of blood apiece, and were humbled, a little bit humiliated, and of course intrigued. We knew we had to return and find those mythical fish.

So it was that we geared up for another go the following May. I remember it was Memorial Day weekend, and I had four days off from the fire tower. Larry hiked in and spent a night on the mountain, and we left straight from there. On the peak that weekend it snowed on my friend M. J., the relief lookout that summer, and her husband Sebastian. Larry and I were low enough in the canyon to suffer only rain as we fished and tried not to wash downstream like a couple of drowned rats. I hadn't brought a tent, only a tarp, so I just barely managed to keep a man-sized piece of ground dry through three days of near constant rain. I began to teach myself to fly fish on that trip, with pointers from Larry. During breaks between storms,

the mountain knows the mountain

and sometimes in spite of them, we picked our way from hole to hole, trying our luck. The weather was awful, but the fishing was fun, a splendid adventure in a stunning place: big Douglas firs and stately white firs in the canyon bottom, impressive old oaks and magisterial ponderosas on the occasional benches, bluffs and hoodoos guarding the place from above like silent sentries—and hardly a hint of any of it from afar. You had to get there to know. You had to be there to see.

I was a pretty bad fly fisherman, as most are who begin from scratch in adulthood. But I loved it so much, I persisted a long while at being bad, until I wasn't quite so bad anymore, then not bad at all though not good either, then maybe sometimes good but never great. Over the years I branched out and fished elsewhere: Black Canyon, the Cold Fork, the Warm Fork, the main Gila. But always I went back to the magic canyon. It felt enchanted to me, primordial, with its old trees, cool shaded bottom, hidden springs, dozens of bear wallows, and forbidding stretch of box canyon littered with boulders the size of utility vans. It's the only stream in the entire mountain range that runs due north. Its uppermost source is the spring on the north face of the mountain, fed by the snow that gathers in the meadow there in winter.

Often as not I went to the canyon alone in the years that followed. It was eight miles from the highway to the first fishing holes, unless you drove in from the west on seventeen miles of bad dirt road to the top of the range and dropped in from there, in which case it was a steep six miles down and a steep six back to the truck. All of which meant it was not merely an enchanted place, but something of a secret, protected from desecration by

postscript

the beer-swilling set. Not the kind of place you typically fished in an afternoon. To really fish it, you had to backpack and stay a while. This was before the 2013 Silver Fire, when there were still trails in the mountains, trails you could follow even if they weren't up to standard.

If you knew how to find a certain spring up a side canyon of the magic canyon, you could tuck yourself away in a place where no one would ever find you. And the fish hardly ever saw an artificial fly, so they were easily fooled and quick to strike. For such a little stream, it held some fighting beauties. Upstream, Rio Grande and Yellowstone cutthroats; downstream, rainbows that had washed in from a flooded pond on the Ladder Ranch; and in between, some mongrels where the different species had interbred and mingled their genetics.

I had been at the lookout five years before I ever made it to the canyon for a gander. I couldn't believe it when I finally saw it. What had I been waiting on? How had I ignored this little paradise in my own backyard?

Thereafter, I got a little goofy about the place. It landed on my private list of holiest of holies, and I went there as often as I could, sometimes backpacking, sometimes just dropping in on the fly if I was feeling super froggy. I drove from Silver City to the crest of the range at dawn, hiked the six miles down to the water, fished upstream and then back downstream, and hoofed it up to the truck to drive home by dusk light. And at the tower on some big-moon nights, I signed off the radio at 5:00 p.m. and half hiked, half ran the six miles down to the falls that marked the barrier to upstream movement of fish. I played along the

the mountain knows the mountain

stream until it got so dark I could no longer see to cast. Then by moonlight I hiked back to the saddle at the head of the canyon and slept under the sky, waking in time to hoof it back to the tower and be in service by 8:00 a.m., no one the wiser that I'd been gone from my post.

In all my times wandering there, I only ever met humans on three occasions. Once, a couple: backpackers, the dude holding a fly rod, wanting to know how far down to the good fishing, the lady looking dubious that this was a good idea. Once, a group of horse people spiked out at my favorite streamside camp spot—three generations of a family, kids and all. Once, a couple of dudes from Albuquerque I'd met some years before at the fire tower when they were on an epic, fifty-mile backpack from Gila Hot Springs to Kingston. They'd arrived just as I was hiking out for days off, so I left the cabin unlocked for them and gave them access to the cistern, a kindness they remembered when we met again nearly a decade later in the magic canyon, kindred wanderers in the wild places.

I went back another time with Larry on a backpack trip. In a place where the canyon boxed up and boulders created deep pools full of healthy fish, not to mention borderline-impassable obstacles, I resolved to pick my way down and give it a go. Larry demurred; it looked too gnarly, he said. I laughed at him and mocked him a little and went on into the mouth of the box, and very shortly afterward, showing off to myself by fancy-casting from the top of a boulder, I lost my balance, slipped, and tore the meniscus in my left knee. We cut the trip short. It was a less than fun hike out the next day—pretty painful going the five miles up

postscript

to the saddle at the head of the canyon, worse coming the five miles down to the truck. But it gave me a good story about the fickle and forbidding nature of the magic canyon. The box was a place of indescribable beauty and not to be trifled with or taken lightly. It chewed me up and spit me out.

For my fortieth birthday in 2012, I wanted only one thing: to drive up to the crest and admire the fall foliage of aspen and oak in the old McKnight burn scar from 1951, and then to camp and fish in the magic canyon. My spouse at the time agreed to go along. We set up our camp in a primo spot where the magic canyon met another major canyon and turned east. I had seen a black-tailed rattlesnake there once, my first such encounter in the Gila, which ever after made the spot special in the way that beautiful places touched by a hint of danger tend to be.

We spent three days and two nights there in something less than connubial bliss. She stayed in the tent, reading and appearing bored, emerging only to smoke cigarettes or drink whisky around the fire at night. I fished and wandered and soaked up the aura of the place like a desiccated sponge. The forbidding bluffs above the canyon bottom. The stunning frequency of the streamside cold springs. And of course the fish. Trout in southern New Mexico! In the Black Range! Indeed, the southernmost trout known to me in the entire Southwest . . . It was almost too good to be true, their presence there. It delighted me anew every time. My wife knew I felt the way I did and made every effort to let me know she did not share the love and was not having a good time, not at all, not one bit. As we hiked back to the vehicle on day three, she in front hiking as fast as she could, as if from the scene of a crime,

the mountain knows the mountain

I knew I would never, ever let anyone spoil something I loved as much as that place, ever again. I would only ever return alone.

Our trip to the magic canyon did a lot to help me understand our union was irrevocably doomed. Six weeks later I packed my essentials in my truck and said adios to my marriage. That last hike together had been a metaphor of sorts for my inability as a partner to keep pace, but then the pace around that time was increasingly set by a burgeoning habit of hoovering Bolivian marching powder through rolled-up twenty-dollar bills, and sometimes you've got to admit you just can't hang.

I never again saw the canyon as lovely as it looked that time. Over the winter my prostate mysteriously went into crisis, and I was so sick I missed several weeks in the fire tower the next spring. Then on June 7, 2013, the Silver Fire started. It changed the canyon forever. Ash flow killed all of the fish, and the giant old Douglas firs along the creek were reduced to charred snags in certain stretches.

I wasn't sure I could bear the changes, and anyway the prostate debacle stretched on in chronic fashion, sapping my strength for backpacking. My health went haywire again on a book tour in 2015, and I spent the next fifteen months in bed. Two hip surgeries. Extended rehab. The years scrolled by, and not until 2018 did I return to take a look at the canyon, having by then stared at burn-severity maps for countless hours, trying to imagine in my mind what had burned hot and what had been spared. Six years I'd been away. But I convinced the guy in charge of trails on the district to let me go survey the canyon and write up a report, GPS some of the trickier spots, the switchbacks and

postscript

rock work, and flag the trail for a crew who would do what it took to reopen it. It was my last mission of the season, after I'd closed up the fire tower.

The journey was in many places an unholy bushwhack. Mile-long stretches of the bottom had indeed burned hot, but then they'd bump up against a swath of the old green forest still intact. Some of the burnt spots were coming back in thorny locust, some in oak, a few higher up in aspen. Along the stream bank, alders were re-establishing themselves, and further down, willows. The place was altered, no doubt, but it was all still beautiful, and wilder than ever, more remote feeling for the difficulty of following the trail.

State game and fish biologists had by then done the necessary work to restore Rio Grande cutthroats to the stream. In one hole I saw tiny fish by the hundreds jumping toward a pour off from the hole above, seeking a way upstream. Further down I tried my fly rod and caught a five-incher with black spots on its sides and the blood-red coloring of Rio Grande cutts. They were coming back strong; in a couple more years there would be mature fish as in days of old. I continued on down the canyon, exploring little nooks and crannies, revisiting Buffalo Soldier graves known by few and visited by fewer, and generally giggling to myself that I was getting paid for this. I wrote up my report. I vowed that as soon as the trail was cleared by the crew following my flagging, I'd be back.

As it happened, my work on that trail survey was for naught. No one never followed up with saws and mattocks and the muscle to wield them. My report and my flagging were soon forgotten by

the mountain knows the mountain

everyone but me. Resigned by the bureaucracy's inaction—another education in the sad fact that the real work of the agency was in preparing for work that never got done—I turned increasingly toward the Warm Fork as my new favorite fishing destination, that and Black Canyon, though of course I still dreamed of the wild, remote, forbidding, and incomparable magic canyon.

Now what it was will live only in dreams. The forest as I knew it there had already been reduced to remnants by the Silver Fire. The Black Fire appears intent on doing away with the remnants.

So here I sit with my memories and my sorrows, sounding like some veteran of a forgotten war, doomed to recall bygone days that smell in the telling like self-aggrandizing bull pucky. I speak like I knew the place, but I really didn't. I never explored it as thoroughly as I wanted to, its nooks and crannies and side canyons. I was always there on a mission: to dance along the stream and play with the trout. It was the best game I knew because you could play it alone—it was always best alone—and you could escape for a while the drag of consciousness through total sensory immersion in the dance. By persisting with it, you could almost learn how to think like a fish.

Tonight the full moon rises blood-red through the smoke off the Black Fire, and on the north-facing slopes of distant peaks to my south, I can pick out spots of open flame in the dark. Week by week and one by one, my most cherished places on this Earth succumb to flame: Black Canyon, Reed's Peak, Rattlesnake Canyon, North Seco Creek, Mimbres Lake, McKnight Canyon—and now the magic canyon, the final and most troubling wound, short of

postscript

the mountain itself catching fire. A burn scar five hundred square miles in extent and growing, and a scar to my psyche I don't even know how to begin to quantify.

I once thought that being the sort of person who loves places more than people offered a built-in insurance policy against disappointment. How could places ever disappoint the way people sometimes do? Places were never capable of malice or greed, hate or duplicity.

> one of those loners
> for whom places trump people
> with rare exceptions

I didn't think to factor in the damage that people can do to places, not just with individual acts of selfishness and stupidity, but by living and burning in aggregate, all eight billion of us in the obscene spectacle of terminal capitalism, so that now all it takes is one jackwagon being careless with a campfire on a windy day in spring, and the next thing you know the campfire is 300,000 acres large, and all the places you love best in the world are scorched.

So yeah: another lighthearted missive for you, my friend. I can imagine your delight in receiving it, the joy it no doubt inspires. You're welcome!

June 15

Eavesdropping on the air operations just now, 9:41 on a Wednesday morning, I heard the pilots discussing the day's plan: lighting the mountain on fire.

Overnight the fire continued east out of the magic canyon and toward the two feeder drainages that funnel off the mountain's north slope. So now the flames are fixing to be at the western base of the mountain by afternoon, if predictions hold. The fire honchos would prefer the fire not make a hot, hard run upslope from below, pushed by wind, so they're going to drop liquid incendiaries in little ping pong balls from helicopters, which will ignite the grass and set the mountain to burning. The idea being that with fire established there on the ground, it will back downslope into the wind at a slower rate and with gentler intensity. It's all very rational, spoken over the radio in calm and decisive terms by men with godlike powers and precisely zero attachment, emotional or otherwise, to the place they're about to burn. To them it's all business, just another day on the job.

Which is probably for the best. But if we're going to light my mountain on fire—my mountain, he says, as if he owns the place—then I'd prefer to be the one with the torch in my hand. Burn it up, let's go for broke, watch the place go up in smoke. Should I not be allowed that?

This morning's weather forecast, read over the radio forty-five minutes after the discussion about burning the mountain, predicts

postscript

moisture moving in beginning tomorrow night (Thursday) and lasting into the weekend, with potential for heavy rain and flash floods.

The timing is almost too perfect. If the plan to burn the mountain from the air goes forward, and the rains come when predicted, they will have come one day late to save it from fire.

June 16

As expected, the mountain burned yesterday. Just after 1:00 p.m., I heard the news over the radio on my air-to-ground frequency. A helicopter was lighting fire at the lookout, allowing it to back westerly toward the main fire: "all structures in good shape," "fire coming down the ridge nice and slow," "backing off the top, burning nicely and doing what it's supposed to do."

The fear, the uncertainty, and the preemptive mourning that have haunted my sleep and troubled my waking hours for weeks, making me irritable, sad, angry, and occasionally bereft of hope—an agonizing wait for what I could not countenance but knew in my bones was inevitable—all of it dissipated upon my learning that the mountain had been set on fire. The thing I had feared was finally here. The uncertainty over whether the place would burn was resolved. The preemptive mourning turned out to

the mountain knows the mountain

be intuitive and useful—time not wasted. The peak was in flames. The burn had lived long enough to bring the mountain into its embrace, or rather cause us to push it into the fire's embrace. The scar now encompasses the peak.

Strangely, today I can reconcile myself to that. Which may just mean that at last, and after great struggle, I am coming around to the tenets of Zen Buddhism. You'd be pleased with me sitting here ruminating on the impermanence of all things, reorienting my vision from "burn scar" to "pyro-renewal." My Buddhism has an untutored, hillbilly flavor. I don't know the mantras and haven't studied the texts the way you have, but I am getting to be an old hand at death and rebirth. I had a vision last night in a dream of eons of fire on the mountain. Trees torching and exploding, grass smoldering, smoke and flame since time immemorial. We know the mountain has burned before, and it will burn again. The burns helped make it beautiful. It burned sometime around 1909, then again in 1951, and again in 2013. The aspens on the north slope emerged from that burn more than a century ago. Some of what burns now will be blackened completely. No matter how it looks, it will be interesting to return to. Even the blackened places will green again, some of them within days or weeks, some in months or years.

The difficulty now is to reconcile myself to the fire's origin in human stupidity. Objectively speaking, the fire should not have happened at all. Lightning, as with the Silver Fire, is one thing. But this—campers being careless with fire when open burning is prohibited in year twenty-two of the worst mega-drought in more than a millennium—is something else: more evidence, as if more were needed, that we still struggle and mostly fail to be

postscript

worthy of this landscape. Every fire we ever suppressed here—we are talking a number in the tens of thousands forest-wide in the twentieth century—gave fuel to this fire that it wouldn't have had otherwise. Beyond fire suppression, we've befouled the place at the edges with mining for shiny metals, overgrazed the rangelands for a century and a half, built roads up and down the mountains and across the mesas, bulldozed stock tanks into drainages, looted and bulldozed archaeological sites, poisoned and trapped and shot the apex predators, hunted the grizzlies to localized extinction, scattered non-native fish in the watersheds to the detriment of natives. It's a wonder the place remains as beautiful as it does. It is big enough and just impervious enough to roads that our endless efforts at unwilding the land have been thwarted. The core of it remains intact. It is a big core, and it is no doubt wild.

What the mountain wants to be now, only time will tell—time and climate. I hope I can have another couple decades of living amidst its wounded splendors as the wounds knit themselves and the scars heal. Whatever it's set to become, I hunger to witness it. The place gave me a reason to live more than once when I couldn't think of any other. It gave me a real home in the world after my original, that farm in Minnesota, was burned to ash and plowed into dirt for a couple more acres of corn and soybeans doused in poisons. It soothed my soul as I worked through the cycles of grief for a brother lost to the violence of his own hand. The least I can do is hang with it through this moment of cataclysm and out the other side. I owe it that much for all the ways it's sustained me. Besides, I've found the only work that seems to suit my irascible temperament.

the mountain knows the mountain

What else can I do? Retreat to Truth or Consequences and sell used cars?

Thank you, amigo, for having the kind of open heart and empathetic ear capable of absorbing such a *cri de coeur*. I needed to let it out, and what better listener than someone who has been to the mountaintop with ashes?

With smoke in my blood and char on my heart, I remain your faithful friend,

phil

acknowledgments

Nina MacLaughlin led me down the path of haiku appreciation with her timely gift of *The Essential Haiku.* Her writerly solidarity has been a blessing. Lee Byrd encouraged my early experiments in haiku and left me blank pages at the end of *A Song for the River* to try a few in print. I admire her as an editor and cherish her as a friend. Bobby Byrd introduced me to the idea of "haiku mind" by having one himself. Gracias, *hermano,* may you soar for eternity on the golden wind. Bill Clark suggested I find a way to share my lookout journals with readers; his friendship and his bookstore, Literarity, have enlivened my intellectual life immeasurably. Writer and editor Marco Roth published an early excerpt from my haibun journals in *n+1,* a magazine whose support of my work has been crucial over the years. The aural historian Jack Loeffler hipped me to the work of his friend John Brandi, whose poems and anthologies gave me much encouragement in the homestretch. Jan Haley, soul sister, met me on the creek with a pack of bad girls when the going got tough. Benjamin Alire Sáenz talked poetry with me for hours in a way no one else could. His own poems light the way toward a music of purpose, a politics of grace. The good people at the University of New Mexico Press are true professionals and a delight to work with. Thank you, each of you, for giving this book a warm and welcoming home.

Mónica Ortiz Uribe inspires me in more ways than I have the space to name. It is my immense good fortune to share the journey with her, *mi amor, mi corazón.*

selected sources

Bashō, Matsuo. *Narrow Road to the Interior: And Other Writings.* Translated by Sam Hamill. Shambhala, 2019. One of many versions of this classic of haibun; also contains a selection of Bashō's haiku and several of his other haibun travelogues.

Berry, Wendell. *A Timbered Choir: The Sabbath Poems, 1979–1997.* Counterpoint, 2012. Written on Sunday mornings after walks through the fields and pastures on his Kentucky farm, and humming with eternal things.

Brandi, John. *At It Again.* Tooth of Time Books, 2015. A beautiful example of modern English haiku from a fellow resident of New Mexico and my pathway into his work as a poet, translator, and anthologist.

Brandi, John, and Dennis Maloney, eds. *The Unswept Path: Contemporary American Haiku.* White Pine Press, 2005. A diverse anthology showcasing the possibilities and permutations of haiku in English.

Buson, Yosa. *Collected Haiku of Yosa Buson.* Translated by W. S. Merwin and Takako Lento. Copper Canyon Press, 2013. A collection of more than eight hundred haiku from a master of the form.

Han Shan. *Cold Mountain Poems: Zen Poems of Han Shan, Shih Te, and Wang Fan-chih.* Translated by J. P. Seaton. Shambhala, 2019. Worth the cover price for Seaton's introductory essay alone and a showcase

the mountain knows the mountain

for the laughter and irreverence so essential to the poetic cohort known as Han Shan.

Hass, Robert, ed. *The Essential Haiku: Versions of Bashō, Buson, & Issa.* Ecco, 1994. The place to start for anyone interested in English versions of the three Japanese masters.

Issa, Kobayashi. *The Spring of My Life.* Translated by Sam Hamill. Shambhala, 2019. Haibun and haiku from the great wandering sufferer of Japanese haiku.

Shiki, Masaoka. *A House By Itself.* Translated by John Brandi and Noriko Kawasaki Martinez. White Pine Press, 2017. Includes the original Japanese alongside English translations of a small selection of Shiki's poems.

Shiki, Masaoka. *Selected Poems.* Translated by Burton Watson. Columbia University Press, 1997. Includes twelve dozen haiku as well as tanka and longer poems.

Snyder, Gary. *The Gary Snyder Reader: Prose, Poetry, and Translations.* Counterpoint, 1999. Represents my earliest encounter with Han Shan in translation and, in certain of Snyder's own poems, a way of seeing the lookout life as worthy of music.

Wright, Richard. *Haiku: The Last Poems of an American Icon.* Arcade Publishing, 1998. The final work of an American original.

contributors

Philip Connors is the author of three previous books: *Fire Season*, *All the Wrong Places*, and *A Song for the River*. His work has won the Southwest Book Award, the National Outdoor Book Award, the Sigurd F. Olson Nature Writing Award, the Reading the West Award for Nonfiction, and the Grand Prize at the Banff Mountain Book Competition. When not living on a mountain, he often has a fly rod in his hand.

Mónica Ortiz Uribe is a journalist whose work has appeared frequently on National Public Radio. She cohosted the podcast *Forgotten: the Women of Juárez* and later worked for the USA Today Network of newspapers, based at the *El Paso Times*. When she's not working, she likes to run rivers and climb mountains.

The two of them live and work, sometimes together, sometimes apart, in the US-Mexico borderlands.

the mountain knows the mountain

Bobby Byrd was cofounder with his wife, Lee Byrd, of Cinco Puntos Press. He wrote many books of poetry, including *Otherwise, My Life is Ordinary*; *On the Transmigration of Souls in El Paso*; *The Price of Doing Business in Mexico*; and *White Panties, Dead Friends*. He died in 2022 after a brief illness, and some of his ashes now live on the mountain.

permissions

"How admirable!" by Matsuo Bashō, "My arm for a pillow" by Yosa Buson, and "Napped half the day" by Kobayashi Issa are from *The Essential Haiku: Versions of Bashō, Buson, and Issa*, edited and with verse translations by Robert Hass. Translation copyright © 1994 by Robert Hass. Used by permission of HarperCollins Publishers, harpercollins.com.

Kobayashi Issa's "Pretending wisdom," is from *The Spring of My Life and Selected Haiku*, translated by Sam Hamill. Translation copyright © 1997 by Sam Hamill. Reprinted by arrangement with The Permissions Company, LLC on behalf of Shambhala Publications Inc., shambhala.com.

Excerpts from Han Shan's #60 ("People laugh at the gnarled remains,") and #74 ("Brown, my face, and white my hair,"), and excerpt from Wang Fan-chih's

#22 ("Money's the thing that ruins humans.") are from *Cold Mountain Poems*, translated by J. P. Seaton. Translation copyright © 2009 by J. P. Seaton. Reprinted by arrangement with The Permissions Company, LLC on behalf of Shambhala Publications Inc., shambhala.com.

Masaoka Shiki's "Didn't burn incense," is from *A House By Itself*, translated by John Brandi and Noriko Kawasaki Martinez. Translation copyright © 2017 by John Brandi and Noriko Kawasaki Martinez. Reprinted by arrangement with White Pine Press, whitepine.org.

Excerpt from Wendell Berry's "The Farm" ("To rest, go to the woods") is from *This Day: Collected and New Sabbath Poems, 1979-2012*. Copyright © 1979 by Wendell Berry. Reprinted by arrangement with The Permissions Company, LLC on behalf of Counterpoint Press, counterpoint-press.com.